WILL THIS BE ON THE TEST?

WILL THIS BE ON THE TEST?

What Your Professors Really Want You to Know about Succeeding in College

DANA T. JOHNSON
With Jennifer E. Price

PRINCETON UNIVERSITY PRESS | PRINCETON AND OXFORD

Copyright © 2019 by Princeton University Press

Published by Princeton University Press
41 William Street, Princeton, New Jersey 08540
6 Oxford Street, Woodstock, Oxfordshire OX20 1TR

press.princeton.edu

Illustrations by Jeremy Tamburello

All Rights Reserved

LCCN 2019931066
ISBN 978-0-691-17953-7

British Library Cataloging-in-Publication Data is available

Editorial: Vickie Kearn, Susannah Shoemaker, and Lauren Bucca
Production Editorial: Kathleen Cioffi
Production: Erin Suydam
Publicity: Sarah Henning-Stout
Copyeditor: Marilyn Campbell

This book has been composed in Adobe Text Pro and Gotham

Printed on acid-free paper. ∞

Printed in the United States of America

10 9 8 7 6 5 4 3 2 1

CONTENTS

Part IV. More Advice for College Success

Part V. Final Words of Wisdom

PREFACE

Over my four decades of teaching, I've noticed many misconceptions on the part of students that affect their ability to be successful in college. Many believe that colleges operate the way high schools do, with teachers who decorate the bulletin boards in their classrooms, check homework, and review intensively to get all of their students to pass the end-of-course exams. But colleges and college professors are different.

If freshmen had a better understanding of the higher education system, they could make more effective use of their four years and thousands of tuition dollars to set themselves up for a lifetime of success. This book is a guide, from the perspective of your professors, about how to get the most out of college courses, create academic relationships, and develop valuable skills for the future.

There are other books that give advice about other aspects of college life, such as how to get along with your roommate or how to manage your college loans. This book focuses on academics, which is the primary reason that colleges exist. A book came out a few years ago called *My Freshman Year: What a Professor Learned by Becoming a Student*. The author, Rebekah Nathan, was an anthropology professor who went undercover as a freshman at the large state university where she taught. As she suspected, she found that students did not understand the process of teaching and learning in the ways instructors wish them to. That's when I realized that a professor can go undercover as a student to see the student perspective, but no college freshman can go undercover as a professor to see the professor's point of view. This book is my attempt to show students the professors' perspective and how we expect our students to perform.

In 1996, I taught a math course for master's students who were preparing to be elementary school teachers. One of the students was a bright young woman, Mindi, who had recently finished her bachelor's degree at a large, prestigious state university. She told me the story of her initial experience there and how she nearly dropped out. She was the first person in her family to go to college. She didn't understand the workings of the college environment and assumed it would be an extension of how high school worked. She was overwhelmed by the complexities. She didn't know how to structure her work without daily deadlines and reminders. Or that she could go to the instructor's office to discuss her concerns about her progress or her cluelessness about expectations. She didn't know other students in her classes, so she felt alone. She didn't know about the support systems offered by the college, such as a writing center or tutoring services. Her response was to crawl into bed and pull the covers over her head.

Mindi was saved by four students who lived on her floor of the dorm. They recognized her plight and pulled her out from under the blankets and helped her figure it all out. Mindi said she was eternally grateful to these friends. We talked about how many other students were in her situation but weren't as lucky. The focus of her high school had been on getting her into college. She said she wished that someone had mentored her to know what to expect once she got there.

Some aspects of Mindi's experience are typical of every student's introduction to college. Until students get familiar with the expectations and customs of the new environment, they can be uncomfortable and feel out of place. College is the on-ramp to a competitive job market where not everyone can be a big winner. Using college to develop professional skills and cultivate relationships with professors whose letters of recommendation are crucial to the next step in life can make a big difference.

The stories and cartoons in this book are all based on my experiences and those of hundreds of other professors from all over the country. Colleagues, both friends and strangers, have shared their stories in academic hallways, at conferences, on airplanes, on Facebook, and via email. I have had many messages with the subject line, "Here's one for your book!" The common thread in their stories is their concern that too many students do not understand the culture and expectations of their college environment—and that this misunderstanding is affecting their academic success.

Our hope is that by reading this book you will be better prepared for the challenges of college classes when you start. If you are clueless, this book will help you get off on the right foot. If you already know a bit about the ropes, it can make you even more accomplished. If you are already in college courses, this book can also help you optimize your efforts. We all want you to be successful while you are in college and for a lifetime afterward.

This book may also be of interest to others, such as parents, professors, college admissions personnel, high school counselors, and others working with students who are college bound. We all share a goal of success for students.

There is a tremendous range of experiences across various colleges. This book will focus on typical experiences at four-year programs. Community colleges sometimes provide more structured support for students than most four-year schools; however, the information in this book is useful for students at all colleges, including two-year programs.

Although this book is based on experiences at American colleges, much of the information is applicable to higher education in other countries. But there are certainly differences in classroom culture and academic expectations in various countries. For non-US students wishing to apply to American colleges or to come to the United States for a study-abroad experience, this book should be especially valuable.

Notes to the reader:

My daughter, Jennifer Price, has written chapters 7 and 12 for this book. She is a biologist and a college instructor with a great deal of experience in teaching online courses.

There is a glossary at the end of this book that defines some academic terms. If you encounter a word that is unfamiliar to you, please check the glossary. Reading the glossary in its entirety may also be a good source of information about college.

Prior to publication, this book was reviewed by high school and college students, professors at a variety of institutions, college admissions personnel, high school counselors, parents, and SAT prep tutors. All were supportive of our mission to provide this sort of good, practical information for college students.

WILL THIS BE ON THE TEST?

Why Are You Going to College?

Not long ago I met a young man who was painting a friend's house. I guessed he was about thirty-seven years old. He was very pleased to tell me that he would be paying off his college loans in a few months, and then he and his fiancée were going to get married and buy a house. I learned that he had only attended college for two and a half years and didn't get a degree. He had spent all that time and money (in school and years more with monthly payments) and had only debt to show for it.

Before you head to college, you need a clear purpose. You should be able to state it. For example, "I'm uncertain about a major, but I am interested in film production or environmental science. I will go to community college for two years to take general requirements. Once I decide on a major, I will transfer to a four-year state school that offers a program that matches my interests." Or, "I would like to major in engineering. I don't know exactly which flavor yet, but I intend to explore the various options by taking courses in different branches of the field." Or, "I would like to become a high school biology teacher so I plan to major in biology and take the courses required for a teaching certificate." Or, "I plan to major in business. My life's dream is to open my own restaurant someday. I hope my courses and an internship in the business world will inform and support me in that plan." Or even, "I want a well-rounded liberal arts education. While I am taking college courses I will explore my options." You can always change your mind, and you probably will, but you should have a tentative plan. You also need a good attitude and determination to reach your goal.

Unlike high school, college is not mandatory. If you don't have a purpose for going now, consider alternate plans. You might work, enlist in the military, or volunteer for a while. Taking a "gap year" is increasingly popular.

> You must sincerely want to be successful in college, not just go because someone else expects you to.

A major source of disappointment for professors is students who are not seriously committed to making the best of their time in school. The National Center for Education Statistics reports only 60 percent of full-time students who began college in 2010 with the intention of achieving a bachelor's degree graduated within six years of entering college. Spending all those years in college is a waste of time if you simply don't know what else to do.

College is also a big financial investment. You can spend $20,000 or more on your first year of college, but if you don't know how to make the investment work for you, it is a waste of money. Would you spend $20,000 on a new car and then drive over nails? Or leave it in the garage for a year? Your college dollars need to be invested wisely.

To make the most of your college experience, you should understand what to expect when you get there. This book is intended to help. It can boost your confidence if you know more about what is expected of you and how to navigate the system to your advantage. If you travel to a foreign country, it is prudent to read a guidebook about that country before you go. Think of college as foreign travel (it can feel rather foreign at first). It is better for you to be informed and forewarned before your college transcript records any stumbles and fumbles.

PART I

GETTING THE BIG PICTURE

Where am I?

CHAPTER 1

It's Not All about You

It was the first day of classes in the fall semester and I was erasing the boards after my calculus class. A student entering for the next class sat down in the front row. I asked him, "Who's the professor for your course?" He told me and then he added, "I'm surprised that in college the professors don't have their own classrooms."

"Hmmm . . . ," I thought. "Clearly this is a freshman, and he doesn't understand how college is different from high school. He doesn't know that college professors don't spend all of their working time in the classroom." Not surprising, though, as we often assume that everything is the same as what we have already experienced.

How Is College Different from High School?

High schools are all about the students. In high school you are scheduled all day into classes. Even your "free periods" and lunch breaks are scheduled. Attendance is taken in every class. If you're absent, you're reported to the attendance office, and a staff member will call your parents if they haven't already called the school to say you will be out that day. There are rules about what you can wear to school. In many schools you can't bring aspirin to school and must go to the nurse's office to get one. You need a note to leave class early and a hall pass to go to the bathroom. Teachers may collect daily homework or pass up and down the aisles to check that you did it. Teachers call your parents if you don't keep up with the homework. If you fail a test, you might be allowed to retake it. If your grade is low you can often boost it with extra-credit work.

The primary responsibility of high school teachers is to teach. They teach a lot, about twenty-five in-class hours a week. Their classroom is their office. High schools and teachers might be rated on how many of the students pass the end-of-year tests. High school teachers try to get to know you pretty well. They might even know your siblings and your parents.

High school is required for most students and teaching them is the sole focus for high school teachers during the school day. New college students might assume that once they start classes, their professors will hover over them in ways that their parents and high school teachers did. But college is not required, and college professors have many responsibilities other than teaching. High school staff members operate as though they are your guardians and colleges assume that you function as an independent adult.

In college, the number of class meetings is far fewer than in high school. Courses for freshmen may be in large lecture halls with hundreds of students. You might not know any of the other students. The instructor might not know you by name. You might have to bring an ID to take an exam.

If you took AP classes in high school, you may feel that you have an insight into how college courses work. But AP courses meet many more hours and have more activities, assignments, teacher support, and explicit information about passing the exam built into the course. College professors will expect much more independence and resourcefulness from you. In high school you might have gotten extensions on some of your work when you were running behind. In college courses the usual policy is "Deadlines are deadlines!"

One of the big differences between high school and college is that the responsibilities of a college professor may not be primarily teaching. Professors may teach only six hours a week. Does this mean that they have lots of extra time to devote to you? Maybe, but usually not. Some colleges are very small—maybe a few hundred to a thousand students. In these, you are more likely to get personal attention. Professors have professional or administrative responsibilities such as being on committees both in their department and college-wide. They might serve in leadership positions for national professional organizations or journals. They also spend a huge amount of time doing research.

The Difference between a College and a University

You may have noticed that some "institutions of higher learning" are called colleges and some are called universities. What's the difference? Colleges usually provide a four-year education that leads to a bachelor's degree. Students working on this degree are called undergraduates. Universities have graduate programs, most commonly master's and doctoral programs, but also specialized professional degrees in subjects such as law (LLD or JD), business (MBA), or medicine (MD). Students in these programs are graduate students. At a university, many professors have responsibilities for teaching and advising graduate students as well as teaching an occasional undergraduate course. Take the example of Harvard College. Founded in 1636, the college is part of Harvard University and offers undergraduate education. With the later addition of graduate education, such as the Kennedy School of Government or the famous law and business schools, Harvard University was formed.

A two-year community college will be closer to the style of high school as there may be more attention to attendance and more safety nets for academic performance. A university, however, will be a huge change in culture for many students, and a four-year college is somewhere in between. A large university is composed of a web of content-specific entities called "schools" or "colleges." These might include a School of Business, College of Agriculture, School of Public Policy, School of Communication, Law School, College of Arts and Sciences (which usually has departments such as English, Chemistry, Kinesiology, Theater Arts, Sociology, etc.). There may also be what are called professional schools—such as law, medicine, or pharmacy—which do not offer courses for undergraduates. If there is a medical school, there is a teaching hospital. There might be more than one campus in the same city since universities are always expanding.

Beyond classrooms for all these programs, there are large support systems. There are vast IT and technology support systems, development offices (they raise money from people outside the university), publication offices, student support programs, dining halls, an office of alumni relations, an admissions office, recreation centers, huge athletic departments (some universities are better known for their sports than their academic programs), a police department, and a post office. Besides a main library, there are departmental libraries for subjects such as music, physics, or agriculture. There might even be an art gallery or a museum.

There are extensive administrative personnel for all of these components. For the academic side of the university there are people with extra duties and titles such as chair, dean, associate dean, provost, vice-provost, and director. They are all professors of something and may be teaching a course or two, but teaching is not their main responsibility. They all have offices and assistants. This means more buildings, so there is a huge maintenance staff and often new construction going on.

Differences between Colleges and Universities

COLLEGE	UNIVERSITY
Four-year school	A collection of schools, one of which is an undergraduate program called a college
Offers only bachelor's degrees	Offers both bachelor's degrees and graduate degrees such as master's degrees or doctoral degrees
All students are undergraduates ("undergrads")	Includes students who are undergraduates and graduate students ("grad students")
Professors may or may not be required to do research in their field of study beyond their teaching responsibilities	Professors must be engaged in significant research
	May include professional schools such as law, business, medicine, or education

What Is Research?

This term is fuzzy for most people. If you want to buy a new laptop, you might "research" laptops on the internet. And when many students are assigned a paper, this is what they think of.

They use their favorite search engine or online library sources to find information on a topic. But real academic research is strenuous work. Professors are not usually hired at universities or prestigious colleges until they have a body of research already published, usually resulting from their graduate school work or earlier work experience. A professor's job requires producing original pieces of work that expand the boundaries of knowledge in their field. Other experts in the field must review the results to judge whether they are substantive and *new*. Then they can be published in an academic journal.

> The responsibilities of a college professor may not be centered on teaching.

Professors in all academic fields do research, not just the ones wearing goggles in labs with beakers. A political scientist might study public opinions in a foreign country to see how they affect the actions of that government and its relationships with the United States. A horticulturalist might be assessing the effect of agricultural chemicals on bee populations. An education professor might be studying the value of homework to math achievement. An engineering lab might be experimenting with how to make an alloy of certain metals that must be strong but lightweight. An English professor might be analyzing poetry of a certain time and place and its relationship to cultural perspectives of the society. A chemist might test materials that could be used to shield space vehicles or humans from cosmic rays. The possibilities are endless.

Sometimes research professors work alone. Or they may work with one or more colleagues, maybe at their own university, but maybe at another university, in another country, or with their grad students or even undergraduate students.

After professors do the research, they need to share the results of their work. They write articles for journals and books that go through a rigorous review process. It is a proud moment for a professor to have a paper or book manuscript accepted for publication.

Faculty members give research talks in their own departments, at other universities, and at conferences. Their publication record can govern their job security, salary, and promotions. High school teachers are usually paid according to an established scale that reflects the highest degree they hold and the number of years they have been teaching. In colleges, there is no set salary scale. Research that is published in peer-reviewed journals makes a big difference in salary and promotion and so faculty spend a lot of time at it. There is an old saying about this—"Publish or perish!"

The balance between research and teaching is different in various departments and for individual faculty members. While some teach more courses, others may be more active in research.

Special Centers, Institutes, Consortiums, Councils, Laboratories (and More)

There may be groups within a university that receive special funding to support activities such as research projects, professional development, and community outreach. They are not departments that offer a major, but organizations designed to promote advanced and collaborative research and particular projects. They may employ graduate students to assist in the research. Here are some examples from the University of Maryland:

- Maryland Population Research Center
- Joint Space Science Institute
- Institute for Philosophy and Public Policy
- Center for Research on Military Organization
- Consortium on Race, Gender, and Ethnicity
- Council on the Environment
- Center for Heritage Resource Studies

What goes on at the centers? Research. The centers design and implement projects that seek answers to questions or problems. Faculty members who are involved with these centers of intellectual activity may teach fewer traditional courses to accommodate their responsibilities in the center.

If you watch television news or commentary programs, you might notice guests who are university professors who are invited to contribute information or opinions. Under the name of the professor, it might say something like "Director, Center for Politics at the University of Virginia." These people are considered the "go-to" experts in their fields.

Who Pays for Research?

The primary means of support for research is grants. A grant is a sum of money that is given to an individual or group to support research. The grants may come from government programs, such as the National Science Foundation or the National Endowment for the Humanities; big corporations, such as ExxonMobil; or privately funded foundations, such as the Howard Hughes Medical Institute.

External funding for research is *big* business at a research university. At large universities hundreds of millions of dollars a year might come from external sources. A professor's grant could pay some of his salary, buy equipment, pay for travel, or hire some help for the project. A percentage of grant money goes directly to the university so the university loves it when professors get grants.

Professors write proposals to apply for these grants. If your professor says she is really busy because she has a grant proposal due soon, she means *really* busy. These grants are competitive and may be essential to an increase in salary, getting a promotion, or remaining employed. If your professor has a grant, it takes a fair amount of time to do the research and manage the administration of the grant as well as write up the results.

Where does a college freshman fit into all of this? College can be a complex web. If you are a new student who is not used to the system, you may feel like a blade of grass on a football field. You need to learn how things work and how to get the attention you need. Read on for some advice.

CHAPTER 2

Just Kidding!
It *Is* All about You

Personal Responsibility

I once had a former calculus student flag me down across the lobby of the main campus library. Tyler ran over and breathlessly told me that he was getting As in all his classes! He said it was because he was doing what I had told his class to do the year before.

"What did I tell you?" I asked in amazement. Had I really stumbled onto a secret for success that was more effective than I knew?

"Do all the homework and don't miss any classes!" he said. "Hmmm . . . , what a secret formula!" I thought.

"And," he added, "I am so sorry that I didn't do it last year in your class, but there were so many clubs to join, new people to meet, late night conversations in the dorms. . . ." Yes, I was sorry too, but not surprised.

You have worked hard to get to college. Once you understand the system you will realize that it is up to you to make the most of your time there. It can be sink or swim. No one is keeping track of you the way they did in high school. There are many rules and expectations in college that are different from high school. It is your job to figure out what they are and use them to guide your efforts.

It may help you to think about the assumptions that you and your professors might have about each other. Here are some examples.

False Assumptions That You Might Make about Your Professors

- Their only responsibility is to teach classes.
- It is their responsibility to tell you everything you need to know and make sure you understand it.
- They all know your name and will take a personal interest in you.
- They will remind you of deadlines.
- They will scaffold every major assignment so that you can inch your way to the final product.
- They will check to see if you completed every homework and reading assignment.
- They will provide an academic safety net and opportunities to recover from fumbles, such as extra credit and extensions on assignments.
- They will review in class for every exam.

Unfortunately for you, these are not valid assumptions. You will be disappointed if you expect all of the supports that you had in high school.

Assumptions That Professors Will Make about You

- You are an adult and can take care of yourself.
- You attend college as your own choice.
- You developed organizational and study skills in high school that will help you be successful in college.
- You will complete all the assignments and readings even if they are not graded.
- You care about learning. You want to learn rather than just "be taught."

If you don't live up to these expectations, your professors will be disappointed. But you don't mean to fall short—you just don't understand the system.

What Do You Need to Do to Be Successful?

You need to do much more *on your own* than you did in high school. This is a key idea that can lead to success in college. The following are some suggestions that can help you.

Locate your classrooms early. Find all your classrooms at least a day before classes start. Most campuses have many large buildings and possibly some strange configurations inside. Make note of the time needed to reach each class so you get there on time. If you are riding a bike, you can scope out the bike racks in advance for each building.

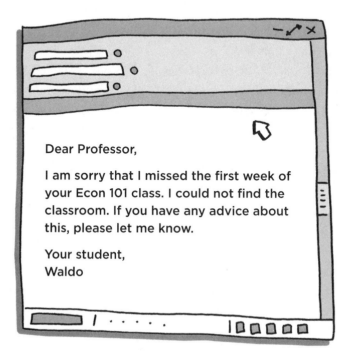

Dear Professor,

I am sorry that I missed the first week of your Econ 101 class. I could not find the classroom. If you have any advice about this, please let me know.

Your student,
Waldo

You do not want to be late on the first day, as you may miss important information about the course. Arrive early and check with another student to make sure you are in the room for the course you are registered for.

Be ready to catch up on your own if you add a class after the first day. Go to see the instructor to introduce yourself and get the syllabus so that you are prepared when you go to class for the first time. This will get you off on a positive note with your professor.

Attend every class. Often attendance is not taken and it is up to you to go or not. Students often think they can read the material rather than attending lectures, or cram at the end of the course, but this doesn't usually work. You are the customer so if you want to pay for classes and not attend, you may. No one will call your parents. But the single most important thing you can do to be successful is go to classes. In my own experience, I have never had a student with a poor attendance record do well in a course.

Read the textbook. Even if the same topics are covered in class, the readings will reinforce and extend your understanding.

Do all assignments and homework. If your college professor does not collect all assigned work, it doesn't mean you don't have to do it. The assignments are designed to assure that if you do them, you will be prepared for work that *is* graded. Since no one is looking over their shoulders, I find college students do not do all the assigned problems, readings, and studying. This works to their disadvantage—not everything that will be on the test will be covered in class.

You need to spend more time outside of class than in class on coursework. College courses have much less class time to cover material than high school courses do. Topics will not be discussed for long periods of time in class, and then reviewed for multiple days. There are not many activities, reports, worksheets, and so on that are completed during class time. You will need to spend your own time completing assignments, reading texts, preparing for class, and reviewing your notes. Make sure you understand what was covered in the previous class before the next class arrives.

Read the syllabus thoroughly. Use it to guide your work and deadlines. Keep a calendar and mark all deadlines. You should not need a reminder to complete any requirement. See chapter 5 for details on the syllabus.

Check all posted announcements. If your instructor posts announcements and assignments on the course web page, you are responsible for reading them and following any directions given.

Go to office hours. Though this is entirely optional, talking with your instructors outside of class can be a big help. It takes some initiative on your part, but it is well worth the effort. See chapter 8 for details on how office hours work.

Form a study group for each class you are in. Meet regularly with at least one study friend in every course. Others may have different perspectives that will help you.

Get notes from a friend if you miss class. If you are absent, get notes, handouts, announcements from your study friend. Don't expect your instructor to help you catch up. Even if you think you have a good excuse for not being in class, you are never excused from knowing what happened during that class. Further, you cannot assume that you will be allowed to make up graded quizzes or labs you missed.

Come to class prepared. Mark the text or homework with comments and be ready with questions. Make class a real learning experience, not just a time to sit and hope to passively soak up some knowledge.

Some instructors use a technique called the "flipped class-room," where students are expected to read a text or watch a video as preparation for class. Then more advanced activities, such as analyzing and applying the material, are done in class. If you have not done the preparation, you will be lost in class. Even if the class is not in "flipped" format, you can still read ahead so that you have a preview of the lecture material.

Bring all the right materials to class. That means paper, pen, calculator, or anything special that the syllabus says you need. In high school your teachers may have provided materials for you, but in college you are on your own. Carry supplies in your backpack. Paper and pen are essential. A few paper clips or a mini stapler help keep things organized.

Follow directions. Read the directions for each assignment before you start. Then reread them when you finish to make sure your work matches the task demanded. Not following directions makes you look disorganized or careless and can affect your grade. If you are marked down for not including a particular element of the assignment, you usually will not be given a chance to resubmit your work.

Start early on long-term assignments. In high school you may have waited until the last minute to write a paper and gotten a reasonable grade on it. But those habits may backfire on you in college courses where expectations may be higher and standards tougher.

Ask for help if you need it. If you start a paper early and need some guidance you can go to your instructor's office hours or the writing center for help. But you can't take advantage of these resources the night before the paper is due.

Learn when and how to ask questions. If you travel to a new place, would you ask for directions? Hopefully so. College courses are worthy of even more questions as they are new territory, too. Even small questions. For example, if the professor says he has a copy of an out-of-print book on reserve at the library and you don't know what "on reserve" means, just ask. If you are timid about asking during class, linger and ask at the conclusion.

Be specific in your questions. You can't just email your instructor the day before a test and say, "I don't understand anything." Ask early. Lay out exactly what you are confused about and show that you have worked on understanding it but you need some help. Do this as soon as you are in trouble and the following assignments will be easier. Otherwise confusions will continue to pile up.

Don't spend time spinning your wheels on work you don't understand. Sometimes personal responsibility means knowing when you are being productive in your work and when you are not. I have students come in and say they spent hours on a problem. More than about fifteen minutes may be unproductive. You need to stop and try something different. Contact a classmate to talk with, go to the tutoring center, or see the instructor.

Be ready to study more outside of class. Don't expect class time to be used for a review session before every test. There may be an optional review session offered by the professor outside of class time. You don't have to go, but it is wise to get there. You may be given a study guide or practice exam, but you might not be given answers. Professors do not want you memorizing answers they have given to you.

A rough rule of thumb for college work: You should be spending two hours outside of class for each hour in class.

Start studying for exams early so that you can find help if you need it. Some professors will not reply to questions sent

by email within a certain number of hours prior to an exam to discourage students from bombarding them with last-minute questions. *Hard work can make you shine.* High SAT scores predict little about your success in college. The students who are the most successful are the organized, conscientious, diligent, and hardworking. When a student says, "I need an A in this class because I am pre-med," my reply is, "You will have to work hard." Successful students do not tell me in advance that they need a good grade nor do they say, "What do I have to do to get an A in this class?" They just do the work conscientiously and earn the good grade.

If you are concerned that you are not doing well and you need to get a certain grade to keep a scholarship or stay off academic probation, you should have a conversation with your instructor. Often she can help you analyze your academic behaviors and give you some suggestions to help you from falling through the cracks. The earlier, the better. After the final grades are assigned, it is too late.

Take advantage of help that is offered. If a professor does offer you a break, make it work for you. If he gives you an extension on a paper and you fail to meet the new deadline, you will not get a break next time. If she offers to read your rough draft if you give it to her three days before it is due and you don't take advantage of this offer, then you should not complain about negative feedback on the final version.

Be careful about blaming others for your shortcomings. At the conclusion of each course, students have the opportunity to give feedback on the course and the instructor. Professors frequently comment that when students do not do well they are more likely to blame others rather than themselves. They may write, "If she had required us to turn in the homework, I would have done it." Or, "He never told us that we needed to proof-read our papers." Or, "She did not remind us of the deadline for the paper." Or, "His tests were too hard." Excuses, such as "my alarm clock didn't go off," "I had a problem with my email," or "I was sick and was not in class for the announcement," are not justifications for failure to meet expectations.

If you start off on the wrong foot, you can recover. There may be a period of adjustment for you in getting used to how things work. You can expect some bumps in the road, but if you are determined to overcome them, you will be fine.

There is a 1973 movie, *The Paper Chase*, in which a beginning law student at Harvard finds himself in an uncomfortable position on the first day of a course called "Contract Law." He is unaware that readings are assigned and posted on a bulletin board in advance of the first class. The professor calls on him to react to a case covered in those readings. He is caught surprised, unprepared, and embarrassed. His options:

a. Complain that it is unreasonable for him to know about the assigned readings before classes have begun.
b. Drop the course.
c. Work hard for the rest of the course to prove to the professor that he is not the slacker that he appeared to be on the first day.

If you said *c*, you are right. You may have these moments in your undergraduate courses, where there will be no coddling and you will need to swim (rather than sink) by your own efforts.

In summary, it is not up to the professor to make you successful in your coursework. Your personal habits of taking responsibility can make or break your college experience. Even though you are paying for the opportunity to get a college degree, there is no customer satisfaction guarantee. What you get out of it will depend on what you put into it. There is a great deal of freedom in college and many enticing distractions, but you need to balance your priorities to put yourself in control of your academic success.

CHAPTER 3

Who Are Your Professors?

I was supervising a student teacher at a local high school. During my first visit to her classroom I took a seat in the back of the room, and she introduced me to the class as her professor who was there to watch her teach. A minute later, the student sitting in front of me turned and whispered, "What's a professor?"

A simple answer to this question is that a professor is an instructor who teaches college courses. The collection of instructors is known as the faculty. A much more complicated answer lies in the next section of this chapter.

Types of Professors

There are many kinds of instructors with different backgrounds, responsibilities, and statuses within a college. They can roughly be divided into two groups, often referred to as "tracks." Here are some common ones.

Tenure track and its three "ranks"	Non-tenure track (no ranks)
Professor (or Full Professor)	Instructor or Lecturer
Associate Professor	Adjunct Professor/ Adjunct Instructor
Assistant Professor	Visiting Assistant Professor

Tenure track: *Tenure* means the professor is a permanent member of the faculty and can be fired only for very serious misconduct. Professors who are on a tenure track spend a number of years (usually about six) trying to get tenure.

Assistant professors are not yet tenured but hope to be some day. This means they are working hard to publish research, get good teaching evaluations, serve on college committees, and attain some recognition in their field in the academic world.

Associate professor rank is usually attained along with tenure through a process that is referred to as "going up for tenure." If the process is not successful and the individual is denied tenure, neither does he get a continuing contract at his institution. This can be devastating. Some might look for a new academic position but often they leave academia and try a new profession. If you know an assistant professor who is going up for tenure soon, understand that she may be quite stressed. Every university and department has different ideas about what the criteria for promotion are so decisions can be subjective. And you thought getting accepted to college was stressful!

Professor (also called "full professor") is the highest rank in the tenure-track line of professors. It is a badge of honor to be promoted to this rank. Usually an outstanding research and publication record, good teaching evaluations, and bringing in grant money are required for this promotion. Even more prestigious is to hold an endowed chair in a department. Not all associate professors become full professors no matter how many years they continue to be employed at the college.

Non-tenure track: Other instructors are on temporary contracts. They may be full time or part time.

The title of instructor or lecturer is usually given to a person who is hired on a yearly contract that may or may not be renewed. An adjunct professor or instructor is a fancy term for "part-time with no benefits." The pay is set by how many courses the person teaches, and these people are generally underpaid and have no job security. They may be asked to teach for only a semester or two. Sometimes an adjunct is a person who is extremely professionally qualified and is brought in to teach one course as an expert, such as when a state legislator teaches a course on public policy or a superintendent from a local school district teaches a course on leadership in education. It could be a retired professor who enjoys teaching and is doing one course "for the fun of it." Or, most commonly these days, it is a person who has not been able to find a full-time position and so teaches whatever courses he can find in order to pay his bills. He often hopes that getting his foot in the door somewhere will lead to a full-time position at that institution. Colleges often hire adjunct faculty to save money—they can cover many more courses with adjuncts for the price of a full-time professor. Adjuncts are not required to be on committees or do research. Their only focus is teaching. This could work to your advantage, but on the flip side, adjunct instructors might not be on campus much outside of class time so they might be harder to find when you need some help. Adjuncts often teach at several different universities or have full-time jobs in other fields in addition to teaching a course.

A visiting assistant professor is not in a position that can lead to tenure. This may be in a temporary position, for example, filling in for someone on leave for the year or being paid through one-time funding. The visitor might stay an additional year, but it is not a long-term position. If you want a letter of recommendation from an adjunct or a visitor, you may not find her at your school the next year so ask for it before the end of the course.

A graduate student may be working as an instructor. At universities there are many grad students who receive financial support in return for some responsibilities. This often entails teaching sections of introductory courses such as freshman composition, college algebra, or science labs. Some schools provide guidance to grad students to help them in teaching but many are on their own.

For the remainder of this book, I will use the terms "instructor," "professor," and "faculty member" interchangeably to mean the person who is teaching your course.

Do you know which of your professors are tenured and which are not?

No, I just thought there are the younger ones and the older ones!

What Should You Call Your Professor?

This can be very confusing. If an instructor has a doctorate (PhD, EdD, etc.) it is always appropriate to call her "Doctor." But not everyone who teaches courses in college has a doctorate. If they don't or you are not sure, calling your instructor "professor" is safe. At some colleges, all faculty members are called "professor."

With luck your instructor will tell you on the first day of class what to call her. Some instructors are very formal and some are quite casual. Faculty may ask grad students to call them by their first names, but it would be a mistake for undergrads to assume they should. The exception is if a professor insists (this is rare). If you are not comfortable with that, it is always acceptable to lean to the more formal side. Do you call your coach by his first name? Or your doctor? Or the police officer who stops you for speeding? Or the judge? Titles are tokens of respect.

One place where first names might work is in labs or small discussion sections that are staffed by grad students. They themselves are students and may not feel comfortable with a title. They will tell you what to call them. They may be close to your age and the environment of the classroom may seem informal, but beware of getting too casual with a teaching assistant. He is still your instructor.

I once heard a complaint from a female grad student who asked the freshmen in her lab if they had any questions. A young man blurted out, "Yes, what's your phone number?" Not only will this kind of behavior get you in trouble in class, but also it might get you fired from a job in your later life. Again, err on the side of formality as it conveys respect.

How Did Your Professor Get to Be One?

Professors have chosen a field of study for which they have a passion and to which they have devoted many years of schooling (maybe six or more) beyond their undergraduate major. When they were students, they were the ones who loved rich classroom discussion, who came prepared for class, who viewed their professors as mentors, who were challenged by the academic environment. They may have sat in the front row of every class and never missed one. They earned good grades or they would not have gotten into graduate school. They did not just get by.

Most college faculty have a "terminal degree," which means the highest degree in their field. In most fields it is a PhD (doctor of philosophy). In fine arts and performing arts a master of fine arts, or MFA, is considered a terminal degree. A master's degree in other areas may qualify instructors in non-tenure track positions.

The majority of your professors are engaged in research in their discipline. They are, in a sense, still students. They don't merely look up information and summarize it. Their mission is to move the boundaries of knowledge forward. Their field of study is not just English, sociology, or art history, but a special slice of the field, such as poetry of the Victorian era, immigration studies, or Italian Renaissance art. The best

> **Professors know and love their subject and they want you to take it seriously too!**

professors are the ones who want to share their passion about these academic subjects with you and the rest of their students. If the CV (academic résumé) of your professor is posted on her web page, take a look at it to see what she has done and what she is working on now.

What Are Your Professors Like as People?

Many instructors hold high expectations for their students in terms of background knowledge, effective study habits, and proficiency in verbal and math skills. They may not appreciate some of the trends in popular culture that spill over into academic work. For example, spelling matters to them. They may be dismayed by inappropriate and overuse of the word "like." The professor may not allow you to use a calculator for a test. You may think these things are old-fashioned, but if you want to succeed, pay attention to the professor's preferences.

The university environment tends to allow professors a flexible workplace culture. There are no standard "business hours" for college instructors. Some arrive on campus very early and some are leisurely about getting there. High schools have some standards of dress for faculty, but not so for colleges. I know one professor who walks the halls in shorts and bare feet no matter what the season. Another wears a sport coat and bow tie every day.

Dedication to helping students varies widely also. One instructor might happily advise student honors projects or schedule special review sessions before exams, even staying late to do so. Unfortunately, there are also professors who are hard to find, even during their office hours. Some return graded papers by the next class meeting, while others are very slow in grading.

Some are sticklers for details, such as never accepting late papers, while others are more flexible. One may allow students to eat breakfast during class, while another may snarl if you unwrap a granola bar.

College culture changes over time. But older professors may not keep up with the new trends, especially relating to technology. I remember the first time a student showed up in my office with a document on a USB flash drive and I didn't know what it was. All of my students had cell phones before I did. I once sent a whole class an email meant for my daughter because I did not understand the new email software. But just because they are not technologically savvy does not mean professors don't know what they are doing in their field.

Younger faculty can seem more approachable and understanding of all your personal idiosyncrasies. But sometimes they are tougher because they want to command the respect that older faculty seem to have. It is not wise to try to endear yourself to younger faculty by inviting them to your fraternity party, no matter how cool or friendly they seem. It is best to maintain some space between student and instructor.

Professors as Teachers

Sometimes a professor really motivates well and explains clearly while others are frustrated when students don't understand everything they say. I once knew a math professor who just copied the textbook onto the chalkboard. Another refused to answer questions. If you don't click with an instructor, it may be because his teaching style does not suit you. Early in the semester you may drop courses and add others, so don't stay too long in a situation you can see is not comfortable for you. You might visit two sections of the same course on the first day of classes to see which section seems to suit your style better. Then try to change your schedule based on what you find.

You will experience many different levels of skill in college teaching. High school teachers may be subject to many requirements that certify them for teaching. With luck, your professor has an intuition about teaching and maybe had some training while in grad school, but there are no certification requirements for teaching at the college level. A graduate student may be an even better instructor than a full professor. Professors at American colleges come from all over the globe. Unlike doctors and lawyers who need to be tested and licensed to practice their profession, the only requirement for college teaching is a graduate degree in the subject matter. Sometimes accents of non-native speakers of English can be challenging. I heard the story of a math professor from Eastern Europe who pronounced certain words in ways that were difficult for students in the class to understand. Then during a class a student figured out one of the words and blurted it out in the middle of class, "Variable! Variable! That's the word!" Class members reacted with high-fives and thumbs-ups. The misunderstanding could have been corrected earlier if a student had politely asked the professor to write the word on the board. But students sometimes think it disrespectful to ask.

Your best bet in dealing with the diverse styles and expectations of college faculty is to pay strict attention at the beginning of each course. Read the syllabus thoroughly (see chapter 5) and follow all the rules you find there. The professor gets the last word, so figure out what the expectations of each are and try to meet them. You should note their preferences and respect them.

In the end, professors are people with highly varied backgrounds and personalities. They can be very interesting, so don't hesitate to talk with them outside of class. Someday you may be asked in a job interview about a professor who inspired or informed your academic or career path. We hope you will be able to think of several that fit that description.

CHAPTER 4

College as a Springboard to the Workplace, the Military, or Graduate School

A student came to my office after a calculus midterm to complain that there were problems on the exam that were not just like problems that had been assigned before. I explained that in the post-college world there is little that will be exactly like anything one did in college. Everything will be an application of skills, knowledge, and abilities that were acquired while in school, but the situations will all be new.

After years of fielding annoying emails and dealing with odd student behaviors, I started asking myself how these things would play out in the workplace. For a while I thought maybe I was being too harsh or that I was not flexible enough to change with the times. However, I have read many articles and have spoken to many employers about their disappointment in the attitudes and habits of young employees.

I found it to be very helpful to translate student behaviors into post-undergrad situations. After all, a bachelor's degree is a stepping-stone to something, so shouldn't we correct behaviors that are inappropriate in that next stage of life? I figured that the workplace, the military, and graduate school would cover most of the destinations for students after graduation.

When students are sending texts during class, I think about how the boss or the client would feel about texting during a meeting. When a student asks for extra-credit opportunities because he does not like his test score, I think about how an army officer would respond to a request for an extra-credit assignment when one of his soldiers does not meet the standard for the biannual physical fitness test. When a student makes calculation mistakes and does not notice that 200 cubic inches is too large to be the volume of a bagel, I think about her working as a graduate student in a research lab where accuracy is critical.

This chapter relates back to the introduction, which talks about knowing one's purpose for attending college. If you look at the big picture of where you are heading, you will understand the need to develop good habits that will pay off in the next stage of life and avoid bad habits that could derail the post-college career.

One of my colleagues often says to her students, "You need to find your mistakes before I do." This also applies to employment, the military, and grad school. In 1999 the Mars Climate Orbiter became disabled in space due to a programming error that used the wrong units of measurement. If a professor is hard on you because you used the wrong units in your homework solution, she is helping you improve your skills and avoid future disasters.

What Do Employers Want?

Once a student, who was a music major, told me about a job interview question: "How many golf carts are in the United States?" She was rattled by the question and thought it was unfair. I talked her through it, suggesting that the purpose of the question was to see how a prospective employee might approach a problem for which she does not know the answer.

There are no multiple-choice tests in the workplace. You will need lots of skills, attitudes, and knowledge that employers

assume were mastered in your college work. Even more than content knowledge, employers want skills that should be developed in college. Here are some examples:

Problem solving. New problems will need to be solved. A dramatic real-life example can be seen in the movie *Apollo 13*. The film documents the 1970 lunar mission where the crew members of the damaged spacecraft were about to expire due to rapidly increasing carbon dioxide levels. With minutes to spare, the ground crew scrambled to design a makeshift filter and describe its construction to the astronauts for on-the-spot manufacture in the space capsule. This was not a problem they had ever seen before, but they figured out a solution and it worked.

Work ethic. Employers want employees who are dedicated to doing a good job and getting it done on time. This may mean putting in extra time and effort. Employers want you to take pride in your work, not just view it as the source of a paycheck.

Conforming to an expected schedule. College students are sometimes sloppy about getting to classes, an on-campus job, or appointments with faculty on time. Timeliness is essential in the workplace. One employer told me, "I want to hire someone who can get out of bed and get to work on time and not just do the work when he wants to." If you run your own business you can set your own schedule, but most people who own their own businesses work longer and harder than anyone else. The military has exact schedules that need to be followed. If you are told to be in formation at 6:30 a.m., you do it. The system cannot work otherwise.

Teamwork. Employers want to hire people who can work on a team. Teamwork is also essential in the military. An army colonel told me, "A squad is only as good as its weakest member."

College students often do not like working in groups. They prefer to maintain control of their own schedule and products. There is much to be learned, however, from interaction with a group. Make the most of these experiences. Be sure to set an early meeting with your group as students have many competing demands on their time as the semester goes on. Meeting in person is best, but video or telephone conferencing can work also.

> **Be open to learning in group settings. Employers are looking for teamwork skills.**

Positive attitude. Students who complain about deadlines and the difficulty of assignments may be disadvantaged in the workplace. If employees make excuses, such as "I did not sleep well last night" or "The expectations are too high on this project," they might not last long on the job. Taking constructive criticism from others is also part of a positive attitude.

Oral communication skills. These might include presentations, expressing ideas in meetings, explaining products to clients, or radio communications while in the field in the military. Conversations in person or on the phone can require good listening in order to be effective.

Writing skills. Make every comment and correction by your college professors a learning experience. Care in revision and proofreading can help. When I read assignments written by students who are studying to be teachers, I correct (in red) spelling, grammar, and usage errors. Since I teach math, sometimes they complain that I am being too hard on them as there is no grade for technical elements in their writing. I explain that when they are practicing teachers, they will be role models for students and will be criticized by parents for flaws in writing. It is far better for you to get feedback from your professor and learn from it than to be corrected by your boss.

Ability to meet deadlines. Employers want self-starters. You will need a set of skills that jump-start the process and get you where you need to go on time. Many college students are masters of procrastination. They can pull an all-nighter at the last minute to meet a deadline, but the product is not always the best. Or they ask for an extension. These habits will not fly in the workplace.

Small deadlines are important also, such as coming to meetings on time without a reminder. This seems like a small part of personal responsibility, but it can pay off in both college and beyond. Keeping a calendar and being punctual, whether you have an appointment to see a professor or a meeting with the boss, make a big difference.

Social skills. Learn your professor's name and use it. In the working world knowing names will pay off for you. Networking is the name of the game once you leave school. Before cell phones, students used to meet their classmates. They would chat before class started and talk on the way out. Now they seem less willing to interact in person. Put the phone down once in a while. Meet your classmates and use their names to say hello when you see them.

Willingness to learn. I have asked job recruiters what they look for in prospective employees. They say they want smart people who have demonstrated that they have the ability to learn and apply their learning to new situations.

This includes being able to learn new technologies on the job. When I was in college, we entered computer code on punch cards that were submitted to a central server. There were no personal computers, word-processing software, spreadsheets, digital cameras, internet, or cell phones. Personal technology meant calculators and they were very expensive. Your post-college lifetime will hold many more technological changes of this magnitude, and you will need to learn to adapt.

Creativity and leadership. Students who want to be told by professors exactly how to do an assignment will be lost in the working world if they need to be constantly given instructions. It is fine to discuss ideas with others, but make sure that you are contributing some of the ideas.

Be prepared. Think ahead. Anticipate what could go wrong. A colleague told me about a student who walked into his office and asked if he could have a piece of paper. The professor asked why he needed one. To do his homework, the student said. My friend was shocked that the student was in an academic building but not equipped to do academic work. Suppose you are in the military and you have to ask a fellow for ammo or batteries because you forgot to bring yours. Or on the job you meet with a client and you don't have a way to write notes about the client's requirements.

Heading to Graduate School?

Grad school admissions are competitive. Only the best students from your undergraduate program will get into a master's or doctoral program. There is some demanding coursework required in these programs, but there is also a lot of independent research, writing, and teaching required. Many grad programs will offer competitive assistantships that cover tuition and some extra compensation. You will need great recommendations from professors to be accepted and to get financial support. If grad school is your goal, you need to be developing and applying all the skills employers want as well as good academic skills.

In order for a professor to recommend you, he will need to know more about you than just your grades. Visit office hours; ask for advice on what courses to take and whether there are internships available in the field. There may also be opportunities in your undergraduate years to work on a research project with a professor so that you get an idea of how you like research and what kinds of ideas you would like to work on. Research experience will also enhance your appeal as an applicant to graduate school.

You might consider working for a few years before heading to graduate school. It will give you a better idea of what your next goals are. After a break from years of school, you will probably appreciate the grad school experience more when you get there.

Keep Your Eyes on the Horizon, Even If
You Don't Know the Exact Path Yet

You may not know what you will be doing once you graduate from college, but your education is intended to prepare you for financial independence. If you treat your college years as your job and do it well, you will be ready for the next step.

Internships are great learning experiences. You can take advantage of the career center on your campus to help you locate some possibilities. Check departmental bulletin boards (physical and virtual) as well. If you are able to engage in these opportunities while you are in college, they will enhance your understanding of various career paths as well as help you develop some of the skills and habits that employers are looking for.

Older college students who have had some work experience and who are no longer supported by their parents tend to appreciate the trajectory of college work to a career more than students who enter college directly from high school. Since they have been self-sufficient in the working world, they tend to have a post-college goal and actively work toward it.

> Think of criticism and suggestions from your professors as mentoring for your future life.

A good instructor will push you, criticize you, and hold you to high standards. Instead of complaining, learn from these experiences; they will help prepare you for the future. Embrace criticism as a chance to improve. You will be investing a lot of money in your college education. It will pay off for you if you learn the lessons the experience offers.

Though you may be taking some courses that you do not see as directly related to your intended career, there is much that can be learned from a broad range of study. You may develop skills, ideas, and ways of thinking that will help you in the future. You just don't know exactly how yet. For example, a friend told me that studying geology taught her quantitative reasoning skills, to think about patterns that cannot be seen by the naked eye, observation skills, analysis of data, and logic and rational reasoning with some creativity and problem solving thrown in. Though she has a degree in geology, she works in advertising technology and those skills pay off.

When you graduate you will need recommendations from professors in order to move to your next stage (see chapter 10). They will write about the skills and habits that you demonstrated while in college. They will be thinking about whether your past performance gives evidence of success in your next endeavor. Make sure you give them some solid evidence to write about, especially a positive work ethic.

PART II

INSIDE YOUR COLLEGE CLASSROOM

CHAPTER 5

The Written Rules of the Classroom

The Syllabus

At the beginning of each course, students receive a document called a syllabus. This may be just a list of the topics and readings that will be studied. But it has come to contain much more information that is crucial to survival in the course.

The syllabus is your course roadmap. It gives you information on course expectations and the consequences for not meeting them. It is your job to read it, understand it, and follow what it says.

A colleague told me that she does not have time to go over her syllabus in detail on the first day of class. She hands it out, instructs the students to read it before the next class, and tells them she will take questions on it then. When the next class arrives, she asks if there are any questions on the syllabus. Yes! "When is the final exam?" "What is your attendance policy?" "When are your office hours?" All of these questions were answered in the syllabus!

What Is in the Syllabus?

Typical information includes:

- The exact title of the course, course number, and section number if there is more than one.

- Contact information for the instructor. This usually includes email address, office location, office hours, and possibly an office phone.
- A description of the course and course objectives.
- Possibly a week-by-week outline of topics that will be covered.
- Required textbooks and other required books with the exact edition needed.
- A list of assignments with due dates. Rubrics for assignments may be included to show you the expected content and standards of quality.
- Weightings of grade components are usually spelled out in the syllabus. For example:
  Two midterms (25%)
  Reading response papers (20%)
  Final exam (30%)
  Class participation (25%)
- Lateness policy for assignments and make-up policy, if one exists.
- Due dates of tests and the date of the final exam, which often takes place outside of classroom hours.
- Labs. If there are labs scheduled for the course, the syllabus may have additional instructions about them. Usually labs cannot be made up as they require special materials and equipment. Missing these may carry more consequences than missing lecture classes, so be sure to note them on your calendar.
- Classroom policies. For example, attendance might be part of a participation grade. Or it might say that calculators may not be used on exams.
- Beyond assigned textbooks, some suggested published resources may be listed. You may not be required to read them but if you are especially interested in the subject or

need more help with the material, you might want to take a look.

- Special resources such as information about a tutoring center or writing center. Don't think these are only for struggling students. Some of the best students use these resources.

Some tips on textbooks. Some textbooks may be available electronically. Be sure to get the ISBN number before you buy a text so you buy the right edition. Suppose the syllabus says, *History of Chinese Medicine*, by Max Li, 7th edition. A student asks, "Can I use the 6th edition?" Usually not. Editions must change by a significant amount (about 20 percent) to be called a new edition. Everyone needs to be "on the same page" so to speak. In a subject such as mathematics, the problem sets are different in various editions. If you buy books before the course starts, make sure they are returnable and keep your receipts. Sometimes when you arrive to your first class, you find that your section of the course will not be using all of them.

Tips on the final exam. The final exam is usually scheduled by the registrar's office, and it is carved in stone. The time may not be the same time of day that your class meets. The room might be different also. Professors might give a final paper instead of a final exam but the paper is generally due at the assigned time for a final exam. Professors are rarely allowed to move the time of the exam unless there is permission from a dean. Most schools are strict about individual students requesting a different time to take the final. You might be required to get approval from both the professor and a dean, so don't leave your request to the last minute. It must be a serious reason (such as having two exams scheduled at the same time), not just to optimize your personal scheduling.

How Can the Syllabus Help You to Be a Successful Student?

You may not agree with the requirements your professor lists, but she makes the rules. You need to learn them and follow them to maximize your grade in the course. Professors usually highlight some aspects of the syllabus on the first day of class.

That is one of the reasons it is important for you to be in class on the first day, on time, so that you hear discussion of expectations of the course. Some professors don't talk about the syllabus, but they do expect you to read it carefully. Some give a quiz on the syllabus, to make students accountable for reading it. If you are nervous about meeting the expectations that are given in the syllabus, you should see the professor right away to discuss whether you should stay in the course.

When you get a new syllabus, read a hard copy carefully using a highlighter or colored pen to mark it up. You are responsible for knowing everything on it. Especially mark the office hours and deadlines for assignments. Your professor may not remind the class about each assignment and deadline that is listed. If he does, it is a courtesy. In your post-college life, your boss will not remind you of every deadline and meeting either.

Mark up a hard copy of your syllabus highlighting:

Office hours
Exam and quiz dates
Final exam date, time, place

Add all deadlines for all classes to your calendar. This will help you identify busy times during the semester, and help you to plan accordingly.

A close reading of the syllabus can give you insights into the pet peeves of the instructor. She may list behaviors that have occurred in the past that annoy her. For example, if the syllabus says, "No papers will be accepted late unless prior approval from the instructor is granted," this means what it says. Keeping track of a late paper and grading it after completing the class set can be a nightmare for the instructor.

The syllabus may say, "*No* cell phones may be used in class for any reason without specific permission of the instructor." I know a business professor who lowers the final grade for every instance of any technology used by a student during class time (cell phone, laptop, or earbuds). He is emphatic about it in his syllabus.

A syllabus may say, "All handwritten responses on exams and lab reports must be completed in blue or black ink." Or, "The use of calculators on exams is not permitted." Suppose you did not read the syllabus well enough to notice the "no calculator" policy in your biology class. You put your TI-84 on the desk (the way you may have done throughout all your math and science classes in high school). Don't be surprised if when the exam starts, your instructor walks by your desk and takes your calculator.

Some of my calculus students used to complain on the end-of-course evaluations that I did not require them to do the homework. "I wish she had required us to do the homework," or, "Because homework was optional, I did not make myself do it. I would have had a better grade if I had done the homework."

These comments were especially irritating to me as students *were* required to do the homework. The syllabus listed problems with due dates. I didn't collect them to grade because students could check answers in the back of the book or buy a solutions manual in which the problems were completely worked out. But since the evaluations were anonymous, I had no way of rebutting these comments.

I then made a clarification in my syllabus to say, "Homework problems are required to be done even though there is no point value listed for homework. I assign the problems that I feel are important for you to understand. I take questions on these problems at the next class, and I give quizzes that are based on those problems. The quizzes are feedback on whether you understand the homework problems." I am sure that some students still didn't do all the problems, but at least they stopped complaining.

If the syllabus lists optional references, you may want to consider citing some of these in any assigned papers. The professor has already alerted you to the fact that these are important, relevant writings on the subject of the course. She will be impressed if you consult those resources.

At any time during the course if you have a policy or expectation question, refer to the syllabus before you ask the professor. The answer may be contained there. Professors are not patient when students ask questions that can be answered by reading the syllabus.

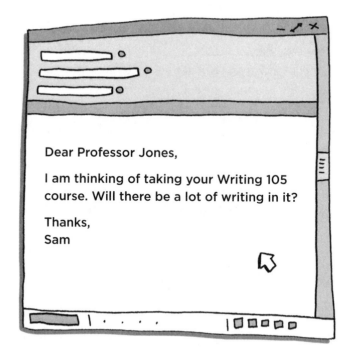

Dear Professor Jones,

I am thinking of taking your Writing 105 course. Will there be a lot of writing in it?

Thanks,
Sam

Some emails may not receive a reply ...

If you know what the instructor expects, then that is what you need to do to be successful. The roadmap for this is the syllabus, so try to use it to your advantage. If anything in the syllabus is not clear to you, ask the professor. He will be impressed that you read it!

Keep a Copy of Every Syllabus

The syllabus is not just a roadmap to your course as you take it, it is also a snapshot of your trip through college. Save a copy of every syllabus you receive, at least until you graduate, and preferably longer. If you transfer to a different program or college, you may need to document the content of a course you have taken because the title of a course does not always give enough information. Graduate schools and professional certifications may ask for the syllabus of particular courses to see if you meet some requirement they are looking for. This could be years after you took the course.

If the syllabus is posted online, copy it into a folder on your hard drive. The course site may not be available once the course is over. It is smart also to print it and save it in a notebook. This notebook can serve as a scrapbook of your progress to date and a summary of your college courses once you graduate. A final transcript will polish off the notebook after graduation.

CHAPTER 6

The Unwritten Rules of the Classroom

Acceptable Classroom Behaviors

During the fall semester, I often get a tentative hand raised in the middle of class with a question. "May I please go to the bathroom?" Sure. You don't need to ask. This is not always clear to freshmen after many years of needing a hall pass to leave the classroom in high school. My only request is that you try to slip out and back as unobtrusively as possible.

Explicit rules of behavior are part of the fabric of high school. In high school attendance and lateness are strictly enforced, teachers have seating charts, there is a dress code, and eating or chewing gum is usually prohibited in classrooms. College professors assume that you are an adult and you operate under the norms of cordial adult society so they give few explicit policies regarding behavior, unless they have had trouble with abuse and feel they need to state a policy in the syllabus. This chapter reveals assumptions instructors make about the culture of the classroom that might not be obvious to students.

Attendance is very important, even if the instructor does not seem to take roll. Some instructors use pop quizzes or call on a random student from the class list to monitor attendance. If there is a sign-in sheet, it is your responsibility to sign each day. Avoid giving flimsy excuses for absence, such as "I won't be in class on Friday because I am going home for the weekend." It signals that the class is not top priority with you. It is better to say nothing unless you have a medical emergency or serious conflict.

I once was approached before one of my calculus classes by a student who wanted to "substitute" for his friend who was registered for the class but was ill. There was no quiz or graded work that day so I told him he was welcome to stay and take notes for his friend. I was impressed with the resourcefulness of the student who could not be there.

Sometimes students suffer from the misconception that because they are behind in their course, they should not come to class until they are caught up. This will put you even more behind. Go to class anyway and resolve to catch up ASAP.

Can you bring a cup of coffee to class? Unless the college has a specific policy of no food and drink in classrooms, you may. In fact, it is usually helpful to students to have something to sip during class. Eating can be a much more distracting activity, so that should be avoided. If you have no time between classes for a meal, bring some food that won't make crunchy noises as you eat.

Be aware that the rules banning food and drink in labs are strict because there can be safety and contamination problems. Some colleges have faced steep fines when the lab safety inspectors find any food waste in the garbage, so please dispose of all food and drink containers before even entering a science lab.

Avoid chewing gum. There is not usually a rule about it, but it is distracting to the professor and does not look professional (especially if you are doing a class presentation). The boss, the general, and your advisor would not like it either.

Can you blurt out an answer to the instructor's question or do you need to be called on? It depends on the style of the instructor and this should reveal itself quickly. If there is any doubt, be cautious and raise your hand.

How often should you answer a question or contribute to the discussion? You should try to contribute something to every class if it is a small enough class for discussion and questioning. Make sure what you have to say is to the point and does not waste time. Be careful about dominating class discussion or being the person who always raises a hand while others never do.

Should you ask questions? Questions from students can be very helpful to the discussion and may help clarify concepts for other students. As part of your preparation for class, you should think of some questions in advance from your readings or homework. In smaller classes when students don't ask questions, I know they have not done their homework or other class preparation. In large lectures it is hard to ask questions. But a brave student asking a well-crafted question will stand out in a positive way. Be specific in your questions so that you don't waste any class time.

What if the instructor makes a mistake in speaking or in a calculation on the board? Do you point it out? It depends on the mistake . . . if it is obvious, such as he says "Iraq" but everyone knows he means "Iran," you just let it ride. However, if he says an insect population increased by a billion and you think it is really a million, politely ask for clarification. In my classes I encourage students to flag anything I say that might be in error. If a student alerts me to a mistake, I know she is paying attention and understanding. "Good work," I say. And I mean it.

Arriving late and leaving early. Both are distractions to the instructor and your classmates. Neither is helpful to you, either. If the disruption is unavoidable, make the least amount of noise and motion possible. Don't let the door slam shut. Unlike high school you don't need a note for lateness or leaving early. If you catch the professor just before class starts to mention why you are leaving early, it is polite. Sit near the exit and slip out.

Arriving late and leaving early should be very rare. If you miss an announcement at the beginning of class, it is your problem. Check with a classmate to see if there were any announcements, handouts, or notes that you missed. A student told me she once arrived late to class the day before a midterm. She missed an announcement that the exam would be open book and that students could bring any materials they wished. When she arrived at the exam she was in a panic realizing how unprepared she was. Forever after, she checked with a classmate whenever she missed any part of a class to see if there was anything she needed to know.

Some caution in planning your schedule may help. If you have back-to-back classes at opposite ends of your campus, it will be very difficult to get to the second one on time, especially as the first one may occasionally run over a bit. If you have an exam in both classes on the same day, it can be very stressful to manage. Being late to an exam does not give you the right to make up the time at the end of the exam period.

There may be consequences for lateness. Professors may give a short quiz every day in the first few minutes of class and not allow you to make it up or have extra time if you arrive in the middle of it. I know of a professor who finds lateness so common and distracting during his 8 a.m. class that he locks the door at 8:05. The students quickly learn to get there on time. Your future boss won't like it either if you are late to work or meetings.

Come prepared with supplies such as notebooks and pencil or pen. You usually do not need to carry your textbooks to class unless the professor tells you to. But take your lab manual or workbooks to labs as they have instructions needed for lab activities.

What is appropriate dress for class? You may dress comfortably, but you should avoid being too informal. I am fine with a T-shirt, jeans, and sneakers, but not sleepwear. If you wear a cap or hood on the way to class, take it off when you arrive and remove your sunglasses. A visiting professor from Europe once asked me, "Why do some students in the United States dress for class as though they are going to the beach?" It gives the impression that the student views the class as a recreational activity. Try to dress in a way that gives a positive impression of yourself and is respectful to your professor and classmates.

In a lab science course there may be a strict dress code. Follow these rules meticulously, as they are for your own safety and the liability of the college. Students wearing open-toed shoes have cut their feet on broken glass, and those with long hair that is not tied back have gotten it tangled in lab equipment.

Label your notebooks, textbooks, calculators, and other property. You are more likely to get them back if you leave something behind. Write your email address in erasable pencil in your textbooks if you want to sell them later. The usual protocol for lost items is to take them to the closest department office in that building or leave them on the desk or podium at the front of the classroom. Check there if you lose something.

Is it acceptable to share a calculator with the student next to you? During class, it is probably fine. During a quiz or exam, it is not.

Body language is important in the classroom. Avoid slouching, putting your head on the desk, or stretching out. I once had two students sitting in the front row holding hands. I don't know who was more distracted by it—me or the other students. These postures would not be acceptable in the workplace either.

Where is the best place to sit? There are usually no assigned seats. The best place to sit is in the front row unless you arrive

late. The professor will notice you and you will be more engaged in the class. Students who are not prepared, who don't want to be called on, or who want to use their laptops for non-class activity try to sit in the back.

Students tend to sit in the same place every time. I recommend that you vary your seat occasionally in order to meet some new classmates. Introduce yourself and talk about the class before or afterward. If you continually text to people from your life off-campus at the expense of meeting those who sit next to you day after day, you are overlooking a tremendous opportunity for support in forming a study group or finding out what you missed during an absence. Who knows, the student sitting next to you might start a company that will employ you in the future. Networking needs to start early.

Be respectful of the classroom. Don't leave evidence that you have been there (pencil marks on the desk, trash, coffee spills, etc.). Dozens of other people will use your seat each week. Unlike a coffee shop, there is no employee cleaning the tables and sweeping the floors between customers.

Avoid side conversations. Whispering between two students when the instructor is lecturing is very distracting to the instructor and other students. A professor may call you out on it with a remark, such as, "Is there a question you would like to ask so we can all hear it?" or, "Please take your conversation out in the hall." If you have a question about the material, raise your hand and ask it. If you are confused about something, other students may be too.

Turn off your phone. Sending or reading texts during class is considered rude. Research also shows that students who use their phones during class for non-class activity, such as texting and checking email, have lower comprehension of class content and lower grades. Even a vibration from a text can create a distraction for the instructor and other students. During an exam or quiz, having a phone in sight may be considered a violation of the honor code. You may be required to zip it into your backpack.

Electronic multitasking in class. Your professor expects your undivided attention. Use of electronic devices is distracting to other students as well as the professor. There may be situations where you are expected to use a laptop in class, but don't open it unless it is required. Taking notes on a laptop is not as effective as taking notes by hand. (See more on note-taking in chapter 11.) Studies also show that students who have a direct view of another student's laptop score lower on tests of class content. Choose a seat away from those who have a laptop open during class.

When you interact with laptops, cell phones, and earbuds it gives the impression to the instructor that you are more concerned with something else and that you don't need to pay attention to him.

You may feel that you are a master at multitasking, but research shows the brain has trouble switching from one task to another, paying adequate attention to each task, organizing memories, and filtering out irrelevant information. College students who multitask frequently in class have lower GPAs than those who don't.

The number-one complaint from professors is that students text on their phones during class.

May you record the class? If you have a special reason to record a class, you need to get permission from your instructor.

Want to bring a friend to class? Occasionally I have a student who has a friend, sibling, or parent he would like to bring to class for a day. You should ask the professor in advance. Otherwise it is like crashing a party. If the professor notices a stranger in the class without prior notice it is very distracting.

Nodding off in class? It happens once in a while. Bring a bottle of cold water, and keep sipping. If you are still sleepy, quietly slip out of the room to go to the washroom and put cold water on your face. Then sneak back in the room.

Wait until the end of class before packing up to leave. Impatient students zipping up their backpacks signals to the professor that they are not paying attention anymore. Classroom etiquette suggests that you wait for the professor to close the

class with some parting words. If he runs over the official class ending time and you have an exam that starts ten minutes later in another building, you may silently slip from your chair and tiptoe out. Otherwise just stay put until the prof stops talking.

Absent professor? Suppose you get to class and the professor does not show up. Unlike high school, where there is always a substitute, college professors do not have to cover their classes with a sub. In this day of immediate electronic communication, if a professor cannot make it to class, a broadcast email should go out. Even if it is last minute, students can check email on their phones when they sense there is a problem. Often the instructor will contact someone from her department to put a note on the door or board of the classroom to announce that class is canceled.

If you get to class and there is no professor and no note, how long do you wait until you leave? You may hear other students say something such as, "There is a fifteen-minute rule." This is folklore. You have nothing to lose by staying and getting some work done or talking to your classmates (yes, please do). If the professor does not show up after about fifteen minutes, take the initiative to visit or call the department office. Someone on the staff may know something about the whereabouts of the professor.

In summary, class time is a concentrated experience that professors rely on to impart their content. All your classroom behaviors should be professional and should support that mission. Avoid any distractions to the professor and the other students. Do your best to come prepared and be an active learner!

CHAPTER 7

The Virtual Classroom

Special Considerations for Online Courses

One of the hottest trends in college education is the increase in the number of online courses. Despite the advantages of this format, there are drawbacks. Studies show the completion rates in face-to-face courses are better than in online sections. Students who are new to the online format may not be a good match to the skills and habits needed to do well in that environment. Students should have a strong desire to succeed, a willingness to start assignments early, and existing good study habits.

If you register for an online course, you don't have to be as concerned about most of the classroom behaviors mentioned in chapter 6. You might wear your pajamas to "class" and eat popcorn. No one may notice if you slip in to a discussion ten minutes late. If your mind wanders during a video lecture, you can watch it again. However, you will need even more discipline about pacing your work than in a traditional class, and you need to dedicate as much time and effort as in classes taught face-to-face.

There are some concerns about online courses beyond student dedication. Some professors may water down their online courses, and there is a worry that students learn less online than they do in the classroom. But colleges are working to ensure that online courses provide experiences comparable to traditional classes.

Types of Online Classes

Be sure to get to know all the rules on the first day of class or before. Print out the syllabus and refer to it often. At some colleges, online courses are made available to students a week or a few days before class starts, so that students can look over the course materials and become familiar with the layout and rules. There are four main formats for courses offered online.

Asynchronous. This means that students have weekly deadlines but flexibility regarding when they watch the lecture videos, complete the assignments, and participate in discussions. This format has obvious advantages for students with varying schedules. It is the most commonly offered format.

Synchronous. There are still a few classes offered in this format. All students must log in at a particular time and perhaps listen to a live lecture. There may even be the option to ask questions in real time. Discussion sections may "meet" at a particular time so that students only have to wait minutes or seconds for a reply from the instructor or a classmate during a discussion. The advantage is that there is more potential for real-time interaction than in an asynchronous class. There is also less tendency to procrastinate if students all attend class at the same time.

Self-paced. These courses have few or no deadlines until the last day of the course. While these allow a lot of flexibility, the tendency to procrastinate is especially harmful in this situation, and these types of classes are now rare due to low success rates.

Hybrid classes. These classes are a combination of face-to-face and online sessions. I've taught a number of hybrid classes in which the lectures are presented online and the labs are completed in person. This gives me a chance to check in with my students, talk to them about their test grades, and find out how things are going in the online portion.

Thinking of Taking an Online Class?
Points to Consider

Take the college training course for online learning. Most colleges with large online programs offer some sort of brief training course addressing readiness for online learning. There may be exercises that teach you how to use various tools in the learning management system (LMS) that will save time and reduce frustration. Colleges report higher success rates among students who complete these courses than among those who don't.

Be familiar with your college's learning management system before you start. If you plan to complete assignments off campus, a high-speed internet connection is essential. All course elements, such as video lectures, assignments, submission of classwork, discussion boards, and grades, will be handled through an LMS such as Blackboard or Canvas. You need to be very familiar with how the system works. It is not the online instructor's job to teach you how to use the LMS. If you forget how to do something, do a quick search for a "how to" video on that topic on YouTube. Choose a recent one, as learning management systems update their features often.

Anticipate technical difficulties. Have a backup computer and working location in case your internet goes down. Most public libraries offer free internet and computers you can use if you can't bring a laptop or yours malfunctions. Start your work early so that when technical problems occur you have time to recover before the deadline. "My computer is broken," "I don't know how to do that," or "The internet wasn't working" are never acceptable excuses for turning in work late. If you need help with a computer issue, contact your college's technical support division. Your instructor may have a few tips but cannot be expected to solve every complex technical problem.

For your first online class, choose a subject that you have done well in. This is the best way to test the waters and increase the likelihood of success. After completing one online course or semester, you can determine if you are ready to take more challenging courses online. *Make sure that your study skills are in great shape.* During the semester before, you should hone your note-taking skills, and practice turning everything in a day or more ahead of schedule. Procrastination is an even bigger problem online than in a traditional class, because students are responsible for even more independent work. You will need to keep your calendar updated and check it frequently.

Expect to do more on your own. One of the most common complaints I get in my online classes is, "There are too many assignments." In a face-to-face version of the class, we complete activities, especially the labs and discussions, in class together. One homework assignment per week doesn't seem like much in a face-to-face class. However, three assignments per week—a lab, a homework assignment, and a discussion board posting—seem overwhelming to many students. These assignments may not take more time than you would spend on them during class, but you are responsible for completing them on your own instead of in class.

Plan your time as if your online class were offered face-to-face. Don't join a bunch of new activities or start a part-time job because of the free time you think you will have when you are not in class. You will need to spend about the same amount of time on the class regardless of the format. The typical rule of thumb (see chapter 2) suggests that you spend at least nine hours a week on a three-credit course. It is a good idea to schedule specific blocks of time throughout the week to make sure that you don't get behind. A face-to-face class forces you to learn some of the material in class every week. Trying to learn it all the week before the test rarely works.

Pacing your work is important. In typical classes with deadlines, assignments may not be posted until a week or so before due dates. Instructors expect students to work on each class weekly, which can benefit the process of learning and memory. A week off from a memory-intensive course, such as a foreign language, can be disastrous.

Instructors can check your online activity to see what you did and when. You may be required to log into the course a minimum number of days per week. Students may lose points if they log in less frequently, and may be dropped from the course due to longer periods of inactivity. Instructors do this to make sure that students participate regularly and tackle the material in manageable chunks. Vacations are not excuses for late work in online classes.

> **Online courses take at least as much time and work as traditional face-to-face courses.**

Procrastination. It is easy to put off the work if you make your own schedule. Waiting until the last minute to turn in an assignment and having the power go out or your computer malfunction can be a disaster when there is no time to fix these issues or find a backup computer.

Follow directions regarding format. If your instructor requests a particular file type, such as docx, jpg, png, or pdf, you need to follow those instructions. Mac users may have to convert their files to a pdf, as there are some learning management systems that won't read Mac files.

Also, be prepared to paste pictures or insert graphs into a single document as the assignment may allow you to upload only one file for a project with multiple elements.

It is your responsibility to make sure your intended formatting remains intact when the instructor opens your file. A pdf file will preserve your formatting, so use it if there is any chance your margins, page breaks, diagrams, or symbols might drift when the instructor opens the file. After you submit the file, click on it to make one more visual check on the appearance of the file.

Order all books and other materials early. You need them by the first day of class. In classes with labs, art studios, or other hands-on components, special materials may be required to complete the class. You may need to download special software or purchase some supplies from local stores.

During the Class: What to Expect

Lecture videos. Formats of online classes vary by instructor, college, and the type of class. In a course that is traditionally delivered in lecture format, your instructor should provide videos to replace lecture time. These may be videos of the actual instructor giving the lecture in a real classroom, a recorded voice-over PowerPoint presentation, or links to videos made by others. If your instructor has chosen to include a video recorded by someone else, don't think he is being lazy. It is possible that he doesn't have access to the appropriate recording software or does not have the resources to close-caption the videos for hearing-impaired students. I like recording my own videos so that I can ask my students to interact with me by answering my questions. Often, I give students tips on how to study and hints about the level of detail necessary for my tests. You won't get this help by just reading the textbook.

Viewing tips. My number-one piece of advice is to schedule a specific time each week to watch the videos in a quiet environment. Take notes exactly as you would in a face-to-face lecture, and don't be distracted by your phone, television, other people, or other websites. After watching the lectures once, read the text and complete all assignments on the topic. If something is still not clear, you can watch the lecture again. One of my students told me that she watched the lectures and took notes, but later as a review, she listened to the lectures again while she cleaned her apartment. What a great time-saving idea! The initial viewing without distractions was really important as the primary learning activity, but the review can cement the ideas and details.

In one recent class, I contacted each student who had earned a low score on the first test to talk about study habits. My first question is always, "Did you watch the videos?" Most of the students with low grades do not watch them all. One student even responded by saying, "What? There are videos?" I advised him to watch every video, to take careful handwritten notes, and to study those notes when preparing for tests as he would in a traditional class. When we talked again after the next test, he was very excited. He said that this time he followed my advice. As a result, he earned a B, the grade he wanted.

Instructional materials for online courses are best when viewed on a larger screen. Plan to complete assignments on a computer rather than a phone or tablet. Many features of a learning management system may malfunction on smaller devices. Some students watch the lecture videos on a wide-screen smart TV. If you will be traveling during an online class, bring a laptop.

Have your notebook handy, and plan to take a lot of notes. If your instructor asks questions or inserts interactive activities into the lecture, pause the videos and do what you are asked to do. This will keep you more engaged. About twenty minutes is the ideal video length. Take a short break if your instructor has posted a longer video.

Distractions can be detrimental in online courses

Discussion-based courses may not include videos. In these courses, assigned readings and activities are required. An online discussion board then facilitates communication among classmates. Although timely submission of all online assignments is important, it is especially critical that you participate in discussions at the assigned time, so that others in the class can read what you wrote and respond while they are working on the same material. Posting after the rest of the class has moved onto new topics is usually of little or no value.

Don't hesitate to reach out to classmates. A regular phone or web conference meeting each week with a study partner can be very motivating and helpful. You can discuss homework assignments, practice presentations on one another, and quiz each other on material before tests.

Interacting with Your Online Instructors

A commonly used slogan in online learning is, "Online does not mean on your own." Don't be shy about contacting the professor, but first check to see if your question is answered in the syllabus, course announcements, or a blast email.

Online instructors are a diverse bunch. They may be on your campus or in a remote location, possibly in a different time zone. When contacting a professor outside of scheduled office hours, it may be appropriate to call, email, or post your question on the discussion board. The syllabus will list the preferred method of contact.

Email is a common means of communication, but allow plenty of time for a response. Check your email and/or course announcements daily. Many online instructors send a weekly email with updates, general feedback on assignments, or tips for upcoming assignments. Sometimes these are sent or posted more often in special situations. "I didn't check my email" or "I didn't log onto the course and see the due date" are not acceptable excuses for late work.

Many instructors want students to post all questions about course content on the discussion board. This enables other students to see the questions and answers, which could be helpful to everyone. Some won't even answer a content-related question by email. If you need to contact a professor regarding a personal issue, use email or the phone, if the instructor allows it. The syllabus may indicate a maximum response time (usually either twenty-four to forty-eight hours) but do not expect help on an assignment if you email a professor an hour before an assignment is due.

If you are local and your professor has office hours on campus, it is a good idea to use them, particularly if you are having trouble navigating the course web page. If there are no face-to-face hours listed, don't expect your instructor to come in just to meet with you. You can politely ask, but since many online instructors are located out of your area, it may not be possible.

There may be set "office hours" during which you can call or web conference with your instructor. Many learning management systems have a live-chat function, but other instructors use programs such as FaceTime or Skype. See the syllabus for information on which program your instructor prefers.

Although some online instructors dislike communicating by phone, others prefer it for complicated questions. If a student is really struggling, has a difficult situation, or many questions, I prefer a call. Sometimes emailing many questions back and forth can take a long time. If a phone number is provided, be sure to check the syllabus for hours that calls are allowed. Assume that the professor is on the same time zone as the college unless otherwise specified. You may want to email first and check with your professor about appropriate times to call. Never call an instructor on a holiday or in the middle of the night.

Few students choose to request letters of recommendation from their online instructors. Most of the time they can get to know their instructors of their face-to-face courses better. Students in fully online programs, however, won't have a choice. It can be hard to distinguish yourself when taking an online class, but a really outstanding project, presentation, or paper could help you stand out. A phone call or a visit to in-person office hours can also help you get to know the instructor better.

Once you are out of school and on the job, you may take professional development courses online or learn a new skill by taking an online course. The experience of having taken one while you are an undergraduate may help you feel comfortable in these future situations.

PART III

COMMUNICATING WITH YOUR PROFESSOR

CHAPTER 8

Office Hours

I once had a freshman in my class who wasn't doing well, and I wrote, "See me" on all of his quizzes. Finally, I stopped him after class to ask why he hadn't come to see me so we could figure out how to help him improve. It turned out that he didn't know how to "see me" because he didn't understand what office hours were.

My student thought that office hours meant these were the only hours that I planned to be in my office. He didn't want to get in my way as he was sure that I had a lot to do during those times. I explained to him that I—and every other professor on every other campus—have time specifically set aside *just for students*. I made sure that he came to my office hours the next day. When he showed up, he stood in my doorway and said, "Wow! Anybody can just show up and ask questions?" They can!

What Are Office Hours?

At most colleges, every instructor is required to hold office hours. They are stated times that act as an "open house" for students to stop by to talk to the instructor for any reason related to the class. You don't have to announce in advance that you are coming during these stated times.

Why Should You Go to Office Hours?

When you were in high school you saw your teachers on a daily or almost daily basis, possibly more than 150 times during a single course. You had plenty of opportunities to ask questions in class and perhaps chat about some interesting topics or problems.

The system is different in college courses. Because most classes meet two or three times per week, this means only thirty to forty-five class meetings in a semester course. Classes might have more than fifty, perhaps even hundreds of students. Many classes are lecture heavy with little opportunity for your instructor to get to know you or for you to ask questions. Go to office hours for this interaction—it is an extension of class.

Instructors often comment that students who are having trouble rarely come to office hours, but then they complain after the final exam that the class was too hard. It is far better to come in early and say, "I am having trouble with this class." Maybe the professor has some tips on how to overcome your difficulties. Is it that the class is "too hard" or that you are not academically prepared to take it? It is better to go to the professor's office hours during the first week of class to talk about it than to suddenly find that it is past the last day to drop a course and that you are stuck with it.

The primary reason to go to office hours is that you need help. Maybe you're struggling with an assignment. Maybe you're studying for an exam and you have questions, especially as most professors do not spend class time reviewing for a test.

If your score on an exam is not consistent with the points that were subtracted and you want to ask about it, or if you do not understand why an answer was wrong, go to office hours. An in-person visit is more productive than an email and your professor is more likely to understand that you care about knowing what was wrong and are not just hoping for a higher grade.

But you also might go to office hours because you are interested in the subject and want to discuss it at more length. Maybe you thought about something in class you want to talk about but there was not time to ask. Or you were too shy to ask in class. It does not matter how small your question is, go ask it. Professors love when their students are interested and curious about their subject. You're in college to learn and this is one of the ways to do it.

Establishing a Relationship with Your Professor

Some professors may not know your name by the end of the course, especially in large introductory classes. But going to office hours may help your instructor get to know you personally. You can talk through course content and your career goals and be more than just a grade in the professor's grade book.

Someday you will need a recommendation. There will come a time when you will need a letter of recommendation—for a job, an internship, a scholarship, or a competitive award nomination. If you cultivate some good relationships with a few of your professors, you will have someone you can ask. Help your professor remember you by going to office hours. It is best to go in person to ask for a recommendation. Even if you email the professor to ask for a letter, plan to follow up with a visit to office hours. (See more on letters of recommendation in chapter 10.)

Go to office hours for

1. extra help,
2. an interesting discussion about class,
3. establishing rapport with your professor.

You can get guidance in your educational or career path. Even though you have an assigned advisor to help you chart your courses, occasionally it is a good idea to get a second opinion or more detailed information about a course. A professor can help you figure out which is the best course to take next. She can help you decide if marketing is the right major for you or recommend a course or an instructor. You may want to meet with the professor teaching the course that you are considering for next semester.

Explain major personal issues. Students can have serious personal problems, beyond sleeping in and missing class, that affect class attendance or work. Professors are usually quite sympathetic to such situations and may be able to help you find some resources to help with the problem. When a professor knows that there are extenuating circumstances that explain your absence or trouble in meeting deadlines, he is much more likely to be flexible with rules that otherwise seem rigid. Meeting in person could be more effective than sending an email.

Choose a future advisor. You might want to do an honors project in your senior year and you will need to ask a professor to be your advisor. If you have established rapport with a professor, this may be easier to arrange.

Why Students Don't Use Office Hours Enough

They don't know what to expect. In addition to students not knowing what office hours are, they may not know how they work. Fear of the unknown is often enough to keep a person from venturing into a new situation or one that is not required. If this is the case for you, try to bring a classmate along. Or initiate your question by email to break the ice. Say something such as, "I am having trouble narrowing down a topic for the next assigned paper. I will come by your office hours this afternoon to talk about it."

One of my daughters told me her fellow college freshmen were intimidated by their professors. Since she had grown up with parents who were professors, she knew lots of professors and knew them to be down-to-earth people. She did not hesitate to go to see her instructors during their office hours. Her friends were in awe that she was so comfortable interacting with professors. You can do it too. Give it a try!

Students may think office hours are only for those who are having trouble. They are doing fine in the course so they don't "need help." This may be true, but even the best students should give professors an opportunity to know them better.

Some students put off going to office hours until they are desperate. However, instructors prefer that office hours are not like visiting an emergency room. Go when you have small questions and you may avoid the feeling of desperation altogether.

Some students are embarrassed that they need help. They think if they just read a little more, look over their class notes, or do a few more problems, the content will all make sense. They are not prepared to ask a good question so they don't want to walk in and look stupid. Sometimes this is because they are behind in the readings, assignments, or problem sets. Working daily on assignments can be a big help. Keep a running list of questions as you study.

Some students believe that email is preferable to face-to-face contact. If your question is short, email is fine. If it requires a long reply, go to office hours, make an appointment, or ask on the way out of class. It is best to ask in person about anything that involves a detailed explanation.

Students are too busy. Sometimes students overschedule their lives with courses, work, activities, and family commitments.

They may barely have time to attend classes and claim office hours don't work with their schedule. You will be making the best use of your higher education dollars if you make an individual appointment when the scheduled office hours don't work for you.

The following is a quiz for you. Choose the best answer.

Which of the following is a professor most likely to conclude if very few students come to office hours?

    a. The work is too easy and no one needs help.

    b. The lectures are so clear that no one needs help.

    c. Students do not like the professor and therefore do not want to come to talk about anything.

    d. Students are procrastinating on the work for the class. They will catch up the day before a quiz or midterm. Then they will show up.

(See my answer at the bottom of the page.)[1]

What to Do If the Professor Looks Busy When You Get to the Office

Let's say you are a bit nervous about talking with your professor in person, one on one. You may think it will expose all your shortcomings. You walk down the hall and as you approach the door you see that the professor is balancing a chemistry equation on the whiteboard with another student. You do not stop because you think you are interrupting. Don't leave! You may politely make your presence known by pausing near the door until the professor sees you. You may be invited to share the

---

1 If you said *d*, you are right. Go to office hours the first time that you find a homework assignment difficult or you don't understand something.

discussion of the problem or the professor may wrap it up and move on to you. He will probably say he'll be with you soon. If so, wait outside the office until you are invited in so you won't interrupt the conversation.

How to Make the Most of Office Hours

Go early in the semester. You don't want to suddenly realize how helpful office hours are when the course is almost over. Go to the office hours of each of your professors at least once in the first half of the semester. Even if you don't have a big concern to talk about, it will make a positive impression that you made the effort to stop by. You can make it brief—ask a question, comment on a discussion from class, or just say something nice such as, "I am really enjoying this course. Do you have a recommendation for the next course in sociology I should take?" If you are having trouble later in the course, you will feel more at ease going to see the professor and you will know where her office is.

Identify yourself. Never assume the professor knows your name when you show up in the office. Introduce yourself with your name and the course you are in. Unless your course is a small seminar, it is challenging for an instructor to put a name to your face and put your face into the right course. You may not realize it now, but you do want your professor to remember you.

Be prepared. Organize your questions before you go to office hours. You should not

> Tip for the first week of classes: Figure out from the syllabus when office hours are for your classes and add them to your calendar. Choose one class and visit office hours the next week. Prepare a few specific questions.

just show up and say, "I don't understand anything" or "What did I miss when I was not in class yesterday?" If you are specific about why you are there, it makes a good impression. Before you ask for help, review your notes, try the homework, do the readings, and make a list of what you need help with.

A student once came to my office hours with colored Post-It™ pointers hanging out of her notebook and textbook. I was impressed as she quickly and systematically flipped to each calculus problem and was able to pinpoint the details she needed to ask about. It was a very productive and efficient visit to my office. You never know how much time you will have with the professor, especially if there are other students waiting outside the door. Ask the most important questions first and be specific.

Don't Abuse Office Hours

Remember that many students may need questions answered. Stick to the purpose of office hours and be careful not to overuse them for things you can figure out on your own.

Professors need to spread their time over all students who ask for it and that could mean 150 or more students. Some students never show up at office hours. But it's not good for a handful to dominate the time that is made available for all to share. When you go to office hours, don't stay too long. Be alert to the cues from your professor. If she seems engaged in talking and there is no one else lingering in the hall, you are probably OK. Otherwise, get to the point of your visit and move along. It is always wise (and polite) to thank the professor for the help.

Don't become too dependent on your professor because you feel insecure about the content. How often is too often to

go to office hours? It depends on the professor and the nature of the questions you ask. If you are showing up twice a week and cannot function without his help, you are expecting too much. You may need to find additional assistance. Some colleges have tutoring centers and that is an excellent resource.

You might also consider hiring a tutor. Your professor may be able to recommend one.

What If You Can't Make Office Hours?

You might have another class that conflicts with the office hours of an instructor or you need help before the next day that office hours are scheduled. Most instructors indicate on their syllabus and on their door that you may make an appointment at another time. Take advantage of this offer.

However, if you do schedule an appointment, you must show up, or reschedule in advance. There are many reasons why you might miss an appointment, but they shouldn't include "I just forgot," or "I had other things I had to do." Always be respectful of your professor's time. She may have made special arrangements to make time to meet you so it is very important you let her know early of any disruptions in the plan. Always call or email in advance to cancel an appointment as soon as you know it will not work for you. If there is a last-minute disruption, send a note of apology as soon as possible and ask to reschedule the meeting.

The Drop-In

Suppose you cannot get to office hours when they are scheduled and you need help. Should you go by the office to see if the instructor is in? You cannot assume that your instructor can see you any time that is convenient for you. It would be better to email and ask if there is a time that is convenient for the professor.

Just because a professor is alone in his office does not mean he is available to help. Professors have a lot of other things to do and so do you. The reason they assign certain hours as "office hours" is so that they can have uninterrupted time to accomplish other things and also spend time with you.

What Should You Do If You Show Up for a Professor's Office Hours and He Is Not There?

Occasionally it happens that you go to a professor's office hours and he is not there. If the door is open but no one is inside, wait outside. It is likely that the professor is nearby and will be right back.

If the door is closed, knock. The professor might be there and tell you to come in. If there is no answer, you might wait a short time to see if the professor shows up. He might be at a meeting and will be back shortly. Study something while you are waiting. This will impress him more than if you are checking email on your phone.

You might also go to the department office and politely say that your professor is not in his office and you hoped to see him during his office hours. The office staff might know something that will tell you whether to hang around or leave. If you leave, you might email the professor to say something such as, "I am sorry I missed you at your office hours today. Would it be possible for me to stop by some time tomorrow before noon to ask you about some issues about formatting references for my paper?"

Learning to Use Office Hours Appropriately May Also Pay Off in Your Post-College Life

If you go to graduate school, appointment times with your advisor need to be used wisely. In the workplace networking is an essential skill and building relationships with your professors can be good practice. Popping into your colleagues' offices can be useful, but you need to respect their need to get work done.

Students who use office hours effectively will get more out of their college experience, so plan to use them!

CHAPTER 9

Email Etiquette

It was the fall semester. It was ten minutes before the first meeting of my Math 112 course. A new email popped into the mailbox on my computer. It said, "I am enrolled in your Math 112 class. I want to apologize in advance in case I am a little late today. I am doing my laundry. I have never done laundry before in my life. I grossly underestimated the drying time. My last load is in the dryer now. I should only be about 5 to 10 minutes late. Sorry again.—Jacob."

I hit delete while mumbling, "Why do I need to know this?" and hurried out the door to class.

In my early days of college teaching, students had two ways to reach a faculty member—phone or a visit to the office. Jacob would never have done either to tell me about his laundry difficulties. If he wanted to apologize for being late, he could have lingered a moment at the end of class to explain. But I did not need an explanation in this situation.

With the advent of email and texting, the phones hardly ring and office hours can be under-attended. It is a good thing that students can email easily to professors; it means they are more likely to be in touch. However, students seem too relaxed about typing every whimsical question, excuse, or ripple of thought to their instructors at any time of the day or night. Before you hit "send," you should ask yourself, "Do I really need to send this?"

Tips for Effective Email Communication

Students habitually think of email as a form of communication they use informally with friends. Learning the style and appropriateness of emails to college instructors can be tricky. The content and style of your emails make an impression on your professors. I am giving you some pointers here to make sure that impression is a good one.

Use the subject line to identify the focus of your email. For example, if you write, "I am looking for a Spanish tutor" on the subject line, it tells the recipient concisely what you are writing about. If your professor needs to locate the email later, he may use the subject line to find your message quickly.

Use an appropriate title to create a greeting. "Dear Professor Smith" or "Hello, Dr. Smith" creates the right level of respect for a professional regardless of age, gender, or race. Use the last name of the professor and take care to spell it correctly. Even if you are older than your professor, you are not a social peer. Avoid "Hey" as many professors are offended by this greeting.

Give the context in which the professor knows you. Mention the name of the course you are writing about and section number, such as ENG 102, section 3. Some professors have multiple sections of the same course.

Get to the point. Avoid rambling such as, "I hope you are having a good day. I am sorry to bother you about this but I asked several people and they did not know the answer. One told me to ask at the library but they did not know either so I thought I would ask you. I hope you don't mind. What I wanted to ask about is can you recommend a Spanish tutor?"

Limit email to important communication. If your question can be answered through your own resourcefulness, take responsibility to find the answer on your own. You might look in the syllabus or ask another student for information that has been imparted earlier. Examples include, "What time does the final exam start?" or, "I am sorry for missing two classes this week. Were there any announcements I need to know about?"

Avoid lengthy excuses for missing class. These appear to be well intentioned, but they are unnecessary and just clog up the professor's inbox. If you are not missing an exam, you don't have to explain why you are not there. If you wish to explain your absence, get to the point. When a student writes something such as, "I am having an issue with my foot so I can't come make it to class today," it can be interpreted in several ways, such as:

a) I have broken a bone and my foot is in a cast.
b) I have a blister.
c) Nothing is wrong. I am just cutting your class.

It is better to give specific information such as, "I sprained my foot. The emergency room doctor recommends that I avoid walking on it until tomorrow. I am sorry to miss class this afternoon, but I will get notes from Ben Smith."

Provide a closing to your message. "Thank you" usually works if you can't think of anything else.

Sign the email with your full name. Sometimes students assume that professors will study their email address to figure out who they are. This would be like expecting the receiver of an unsigned letter to look for the return address on the envelope to see who sent it. Email addresses may not match the current name of the student. Martha Custis may have been issued the email address mcustis@xxxx.edu as a freshman, but finished her education under the name Martha Washington. The college does not usually issue a new email address so her name may not be evident by looking at the name of the sender.

Hey, what did I miss in class today?

The email all professors hate

Use your college email address. Faculty sometimes do blast emails from the college software program. Messages will be sent to the address issued to you by the college. Some colleges forbid faculty from corresponding with students using any address other than a student's college address, so be sure to use this address for outgoing messages as well. Check your college email daily. If you use your college email address exclusively for your school correspondence, you will have it all in one mailbox. Saying that you didn't see the message is not an excuse for not knowing what is going on.

When a professor initiates an email to you, be sure to reply. If she sends an email that is sent only to you rather than the whole class, you need to reply. For example, if the professor writes, "The paper you turned in yesterday seems to be missing the required tables," common courtesy requires a reply. Be responsive to all messages and let your professor be the one to stop replying. If the email sounds like a wellness check such as, "You missed the midterm this morning. Are you all right?" and you don't reply within twenty-four hours or so, the professor may call the Dean of Students office to have someone check on you.

Your emails make an impression. Slang, emojis, abbreviations, and text message style are not appropriate in emailing your professor. They won't fly on a job application either! Correct spelling, punctuation, and word choices make a difference. Treat each email as a "business letter" rather than a "friendly letter" in tone.

> **Think of email with your instructors as a professional interaction.**

Think before you send an email. You do not want to appear helpless and too dependent. If your email has a tone of "I was just wondering . . . ," you probably don't need to send it. Here are some examples of messages that are worth sending and receiving.

- "Do you have time to see me on Thursday afternoon at 4:00? I have several questions about mistakes I made on the midterm that I would like advice about."
- "I do not want you to think that I am neglecting your class today. I have a bad case of food poisoning. The health center has advised me to stay home for at least 24 hours. Sara Hall is sharing her notes from today's class with me. So hopefully I will be back on track by Monday both physically and academically."

- "The list of homework problems includes #65 on page 432. But there is no problem 65 on that page. Just letting you know in case you had a different problem in mind."
- "Thank you for writing the letter of recommendation for me. I got the scholarship!"

Reread your email before you hit "send." Proofreading will increase the probability that your message is clear and mechanically sound. Sloppiness makes an impression. If you intend to attach a file, make sure you actually do it.

How soon can you expect a response? There is an expression used in college culture, "Email is not a professor's friend!" There can be such a large volume of messages that

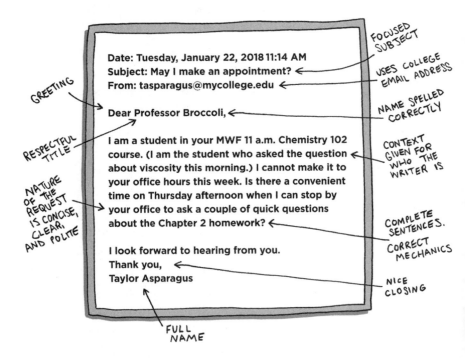

Example of an ideal email

it is intimidating for an instructor to log onto email first thing in the morning. Do not expect that your instructor is eagerly waiting for the ping of student emails and will provide an immediate response.

Assume that your professors do not check email 24/7. Expect email correspondence to be answered during business hours. Consider it a bonus if it gets answered outside of those hours. If you send an email on Friday, it is not a good idea to write again on Sunday and complain that you did not get a reply.

If you don't get a reply to something truly important within twenty-four hours, you might try calling the professor's office or going by in person. This means you need to get moving early on all assignments so you have the cushion of time when problems arise.

Email versus Visiting the Office in Person

You may be used to doing everything online—shopping, banking, renewing a driver's license, and you may be more comfortable online than in person. But there are many situations that need handling in person.

Email can create a layer of impersonality between instructor and student. I often prefer to see and hear my students. I get to know them better and on complex issues I can help them better.

Only simple things are handled well via email. "May I stop by your office today at 2:00 to pick up my quiz?" is fine for email. "Do I belong in this course?" is a question that requires some discussion in person. If you cannot get to the point in a couple of sentences, it may be a situation that needs an in-person visit to the office.

Suppose you want help with a math or engineering problem that requires many lines of symbols or diagrams. This is done more easily in person. You will benefit from some discussion, not just an answer.

If you have a personal problem you want to discuss, go to see the instructor in her office. Problems with your health, your roommate, depression, or your family are common and legitimate distractions from your academic work. I prefer that students do not put anything personal in writing, including grades, if they do not want it known by more than the intended recipient. I never consider email private.

Complaints are handled better in person. A student named Dan told me he sent an email to his professor complaining that the expectations in the course were too great. The professor wrote, "Come to see me." He did and they had a good discussion that helped Dan appreciate the point of view of the professor. You can't do that well via email. Then the professor said, "Now let's talk about the tone of your email." And Dan learned from that discussion also!

If you must complain by email, find a way to turn it into a concern rather than a rant. Think about what you would say in person, which tends to be more polite and constructive. Instead of "The amount of homework in this course is outrageous!" you might try "I am having trouble getting assignments done on time. The amount of homework is a lot for me." No matter how polite you are, the professor is likely to ask you to come to the office in person to discuss this and figure out a way to help you.

I believe that many complaints made via email would not be made if a student had to come in person to the office to talk. It is easy to sit in your room at midnight and type a complaint. "I thought the test today was much too long and unfair!" seems more like a comment on Facebook than a discussion starter with the instructor.

Do you want to shine? Surprise your professors once in a while by sending an email that is complimentary. For example, you could say, "Thank you for staying after class today to answer my questions. It really got me back on track."

Email should be professional communication that succinctly and respectfully conveys important information. Learning to do that is part of your training for post-college life. It will pay off tremendously if you get into good habits now.

CHAPTER 10

Letters of Recommendation

A student once asked me for a letter of recommendation for a corporate internship she was applying for. There was not much time until it was due so I wrote the letter right away. Then the company never contacted me with a link to the site where the letter was to be uploaded. The next time I saw the student, I asked what happened. She said she decided not to apply after all. I was surprised she had not told me as soon as she changed the plan. She did not seem to understand how much trouble it was for me to try to help her on short notice and have my efforts rendered unnecessary. A year later she asked me for a letter in support of her graduate school application. I felt I could not write a good one given what had happened the first time.

A Letter of Recommendation Is a Type of Performance Review

Your time in college is your time for building experience, practicing your skills, and demonstrating your personal qualities. No one will make up good things to say about you. It would reflect poorly on the recommenders if you turn out to be a disappointment once you land the job or graduate school position. It is your job to build the substance of your academic record and to make sure several of your instructors know you and your record well enough to comfortably recommend you. If you have read the other chapters in this book, you have an idea of what will make you shine in a letter of recommendation. Now you need to know how the recommending process works.

Asking for a Recommendation

Every student will need a recommendation for something. While you are still a student you might need a recommendation for a summer job, an internship, a transfer application, a scholarship, or support for an award. When you are close to graduating, you will need recommendations for the next step in your life—employment and graduate school are the most common.

How do you decide which professors to ask for a letter? You should ask the professors who know you best and who have the most positive and interesting things to say about you. They will be familiar with your intellectual development and your skills as well as your personal qualities. Don't ask a professor to write a recommendation unless you are sure it will be a positive one. Professors will not write a positive letter just to be nice.

You might start by sending an email to a professor to ask politely if he feels comfortable recommending you and has the time to do it. Give the deadline and briefly say what the recommendation is for. It is easier for a professor to decline in an email response than if you are sitting in the office. You don't want to beg for a recommendation. You want it to come with some enthusiasm.

You might mention why you think the professor would be a good person to do this for you. For example, "Since I worked on your summer research project I was hoping you would be willing to comment on my interest and experience in research as I am applying for graduate school."

Contact the professors early. You may need two or three professors to recommend you. When you ask for a recommendation you need to do it at least a month before the deadline. It is time-consuming for these recommendations to be completed. A short lead time may not result in the quality of the letter you hope will be written.

After your email request, make an appointment to see each professor in person. Give some details of what your goals are, such as graduate school, employment, an internship, or a scholarship, as the slant on the letter may be different depending on who will be reading it. If you need recommendations submitted to multiple places, which is common when applying to grad schools and jobs, bring a list of where you are applying, due dates, and any information about how the recommendation is to be submitted.

Most recommendations are submitted online. But if you need hard copies mailed out, provide addressed envelopes with stamps on them. Or give the professor address labels and stamps to put on her departmental letterhead envelope. If you are required to submit a paper form, print the form, fill out your required parts, and sign it before delivering it to the professor.

> Your high school teachers probably knew you well. In college, you need to work harder at getting to know a professor well enough for her to write a recommendation for you.

If you are asked on an application to list some professors who can be contacted for a recommendation, be sure to ask each one before you put any names down. They need to know they will be contacted, especially if the contact comes via email. Email from an unknown sender might go to spam or be overlooked by the receiver if it is not expected.

Should you ask for your own copy of a recommendation? Some professors may allow you to read the letter, but it is rare. Students usually have the opportunity to sign a waiver that says they agree not to see the recommendation. I don't write recommendations for anyone unless he or she waives the right to see what I write. The receiver of the recommendation may take it more seriously if he knows I am being candid. If a student needs a letter to insert in an application packet, I put it in a sealed envelope and sign across the seal in the back.

It is best to get the recommendation when you are fresh in the professor's mind. If it has been a couple of years since you have had contact with a professor, it is harder for her to recommend you. Maybe you took only one course from this professor. If some time has passed, it is harder for her to think of the right details to mention. It's in your best interests to maintain some contact with a professor who knows you well after your course ends to keep her updated on your progress and plans.

I once had a student come to my office to ask for a recommendation for officer training in the Marine Corps. It had been two years since he was in a course with me. I remembered a lot about him but I drew a blank on his name as he was standing in my doorway. He was in a hurry and dashed off to class, telling me he would drop off a form later in the week. He then dropped off the form but neglected to fill in his name! Fortunately, I had asked him to email me a week before it was due to nudge me to get it done. He did and he signed his email. My letter must have been good enough to get him in as he invited me to his commissioning ceremony.

Another student wrote me while he was out of the country for a study-abroad program. He attached a photo of himself since he couldn't come to my office in person. I remembered him well because he was an outstanding student who contributed much to my class. He was smart to send the photo to ensure that I didn't confuse him with another student.

Ask before you graduate. If I write a letter for a student, I store it on my computer. If a request comes later, I can adapt the letter without too much trouble. But if the application requires responses to specific questions, it is harder once some time has gone by. I had a student named Jessica Smith (not a unique name) write me three years after graduation to ask for a recommendation. "Hmmm . . . ," I thought, "was she the student who usually sat in the front row and did the presentation on transcendental numbers, or was she the one who sat on the left side and did the presentation on density of primes?" If she had come into my office asking for this favor, I would have been able to trigger some details of her performance. I declined to recommend her as I could not reliably pull up the memories.

Develop a Solid Record and Positive Relationships with Your Professors Early

How does a professor get to know you well? It is difficult to write about a student who was just "present" in classes. The challenge for you is to provide the professor with direct evidence of your skills and accomplishments. A professor's recommendation must show insights beyond what is stated on your transcript. You need to take the initiative to make yourself and your skills known.

You can begin by participating fully in classes and doing excellent work on your assignments. These things get you noticed. Then go to office hours, especially for a professor whom you are likely to ask for a recommendation.

By the end of your second year, you need to choose an adviser from the department of your major. It is probably someone who taught one or more of your courses. Over the next two years, the adviser should get to know you even better as you plan for future courses.

Seek out opportunities to participate in a professor's research project, work as a grader, or do a senior paper with a faculty adviser. These experiences will provide a good context for the professor to get to know you and will provide good insights for a recommendation.

Sometimes students give me a copy of their résumé, but it is not necessary. The student will provide the résumé directly as part of the application. They may want me to see all their extracurricular activities. It does not help me write a letter because I will write only about what I know directly. It is not appropriate for me to say anything about a student's being on the soccer team. The soccer coach can write that letter. If I know that a student did an internship and we have discussed an interesting problem she worked on while there, I might give my insights about her work ethic and problem-solving abilities based on our discussion. But if I only know she did the internship because I see it on the résumé, it is not appropriate for me to mention it in my letter.

You need to distinguish yourself. Many of the applications require the recommender to rate the applicant on specific characteristics by comparing you to others such as all students the instructor has ever taught in her course (top 10%, top 25%, top 50%, lower 50%, etc.). This means that you need to distinguish yourself to look good. If you aren't actively demonstrating your skills, your professor won't have information to support a good recommendation.

The questionnaires vary but they may include rating qualities such as analytical ability, oral communication skills, written

communication skills, interpersonal skills, ability to work well in a group, receptivity to feedback, emotional maturity, creativity, resourcefulness, motivation, record of meeting deadlines, leadership qualities, and independence. You might think about how you can make your assets in these areas known to your professors during your time in their classes so that when recommendation time comes, they have plenty of positive things to say.

If you were not an A student, can you still ask to be recommended? There are ways to distinguish yourself besides grades. I once had a freshman calculus student who was not a strong student mathematically, partly due to a poor background in algebra. He earned a C in my course. He came to my office hours often so I got to know him well during the time I was helping him. He visited my office during his senior year and asked me to write a recommendation for him for a job application. He said he knew his grade was mediocre, but he felt that I understood some things about him that might not come through in his grades. Yes, I did. I knew of his work ethic, his ability to ask questions, his persistence at trying to understand concepts and solve problems, and his positive attitude. He had an ability to work with others, an enthusiasm for learning the concepts rather than just getting the grade, and a perfect attendance record. I wrote him a nice letter explaining all of that. There is much more information conveyed in a letter than grades alone that may impress an employer.

Few More Things You Should Consider

What should you do if the recommendation is not sent? You can usually track the progress of your applications. If you become aware that a recommendation has not been sent and it is near the deadline, send a polite email to the professor to say it has not been received. Professors are very busy and these things can unintentionally fall by the wayside. They will appreciate a reminder.

Be careful not to ask one professor to write too many letters. Most recommendations are electronic and the professor is sent a link to an online questionnaire as well as a request for a letter to be attached. They all have different formats and deadlines. It becomes a matrix of responsibility that is hard to keep up with. Once a professor writes a letter and stores it on his computer, it is easy to retrieve it for more recommendation requests. It may need to be tailored for each new application as some places ask for specific feedback. The list of questions is different at all the electronic sites so the marginal amount of work to submit each different one is not trivial. If a student is applying to fifteen graduate schools, it can be a daunting task to get the recommendations done. Remember that the professor is doing you a favor so don't overdo it.

Say thank you. When you ask for a recommendation, you are asking for a favor. Even though it is part of the job of the instructor, it is not the easiest add-on to the workday. Always thank the recommender. An emailed note of gratitude is fine, but a handwritten note in the professor's mailbox is a real treat. We would love to hear how your application or quest turned out so include that information if you can.

Are gifts appropriate? I once received a note of thanks for writing a recommendation. Inside the card was a $20 gift card for a bookstore. I returned it to the student, saying that I appreciated the generous thought, but that it is part of my job to write recommendations. Token gifts that show up at random times are appreciated by professors—for example, a jar of cranberry jam from a student who brought it from his home state of Maine, a homemade bookmark, or a small box of holiday cookies. The gift should be given in the tone of "I enjoyed your course" rather than for writing a recommendation. A note of thanks for the recommendation is enough.

My recommendation to you: During your freshman year, draft the letter you hope someone will write about you when you graduate. Update it each year. If all goes well you will add new dimensions to your exhibited skills and talents each year. You can make it easy for professors to recommend you if you live up to the plan you have envisioned for yourself.

PART IV

MORE ADVICE FOR COLLEGE SUCCESS

CHAPTER 11

Getting the Best Grades You Can

About the second week of classes I have anxious freshmen, sometimes with tears in their eyes, come to my office because they did not do well on the first quiz. They are sure it is a sign of failure. They were A students in high school! I calm them down and give them my best advice and reassurance that things will get better. And it usually does get better.

Why do good grades seem harder to achieve in college? The task demands may be harder, the competition may be stiffer, and distractions are everywhere in college. Students sometimes think that if they just complete the assignments, they will get a good grade. Being "present" in class and turning in assignments on time are not enough. Good grades need to be earned by you, not given by your professors. In work that is graded subjectively, the top grades are reserved for the best responses, performance, or papers submitted. It takes hard work and self-discipline with less guidance than some students are used to. You may find yourself in a course that weights midterms and the final exam for the bulk of the grade. This is a hard adjustment for some college freshmen when they are used to many regular quizzes in high school courses that can boost their performance overall.

Exams may seem harder than you expect. However, sometimes they are designed so that no one gets a high percentage of correct answers and the exams are graded on a curve. One student told me how upset she was about getting a score of 58 percent on an exam until she found out that was a grade of B+.

If you were at the top of your class in high school, don't be too disappointed if your college grades are not as good. It may take you a while to get the feel for how to do your best in a new environment. A few Bs and Cs are not going to ruin your career. Don't sweat too much if you are not perfect. Nobody is.

Recipe for Maximizing Your Grades

Study early and often. It is rare that professors spend class time reviewing for a quiz or an exam so you need to find a way to structure your own studying. The most successful students study continuously over the course with more emphasis just before the exam. The length of time you study just before a test is not directly proportional to the grade you will get. Students sometimes say, "But I studied so hard for this test!" when they are disappointed about the result. The problem may be waiting until the day before an exam to do any studying. If you study well in advance of the exam, you have time to get help if you need it. Go to bed at a reasonable time the night before the exam. Sometimes a good night's sleep pays off more than studying all night.

Take notes in class. Even if the professor posts the Power-Points on the course web page, take notes anyway. It keeps you focused and contributes to storing and processing information. Printing the PowerPoint presentation ahead of time and taking notes in the margins is not recommended, as it does not keep you engaged to the same extent. Instructors (and other students) may be annoyed if you snap photos of the board or PowerPoints.

Take your notes by hand rather than on a laptop. Don't try to write everything down. Students who use a laptop tend to transcribe the whole lecture, which can interfere with the brain's ability to encode new information. Those who write by hand are engaged with selecting the most important points and summarizing. Brain research shows that people process information better while writing by hand. Pam Mueller of Princeton University and Daniel Oppenheimer of UCLA found that students who took notes by hand performed better on both recall and conceptual questions.

Review your notes within forty-eight hours of taking them. If you copy any formulas or definitions in class, check them in your text materials before you memorize them. If there is anything in them that seems confusing, go to your instructor's office hours to ask. Don't wait until you need to study for a test.

Form a study group. Students who work together can help each other and discuss concepts. The classroom does not give everyone a chance to talk and get feedback, but a study group does. When you explain something to a friend in the group, it helps you cement your own understanding. You may also gain insights from the perspectives of others. By scheduling meetings of your group, you help pace your work.

Identify key concepts. Prepare yourself to explain them, not just hope you can find them in a multiple-choice list. You need to develop a deep understanding of the material, not just memorize facts. College courses emphasize higher-level thinking.

Follow directions. Revisit the directions for every assignment to make sure you have met the expectations. Sometimes students complain about a grade by saying they did not know they had to include certain components. It may be that expectations were listed in the assignment or in a rubric (a guide for specific elements of scoring), but the student did not read it or follow it. Consult the syllabus frequently to remind yourself of the requirements, deadlines, and procedures.

If you are unsure of what is meant by any part of an assignment, ask. It might be best to go to office hours for in-person clarification. You will start out more confidently if you are sure of what the expectations are.

If no rubric is given, there still may be one in the head of the professor when she grades. It may range from a low score for minimal evidence of a correct response to full credit for a brilliant response that goes beyond what is expected. Adequate is not enough in most professor's grading schemes to merit a good score.

Meet the deadlines. Mark your calendar for each exam date and assignment deadline. Students often make the mistake of only working on the next thing that is due. Look ahead to the big, long-term assignments and set your own intermediate deadlines.

Do all assigned reading and homework assignments even if they are not graded. The assignments are given with a purpose. They will prepare you for better scores on the items that *are* graded. In technical courses such as math, don't just try to find the answer. Learn the concept and process so that when you get a new problem, you can approach it with confidence.

Know everything from your quizzes and midterms before you take the final exam. Figure out what you did wrong on earlier assessments as soon as they are returned to you. Then review them for the final exam.

Answer every question on an exam. Show what you know. You may get partial credit for some correct information even if it is not a complete answer.

Go to see your professor at the first sign of trouble. Go with specific questions about where you need help. This means you have to do some work before you go. You may be able to identify ways that you can optimize your future performance.

Other Tips Relating to Grades

Extra credit. I am often asked by students if there is a way they can do an extra-credit assignment to bring up a grade. The simple answer is no. A student told me extra credit is how she got through high school. She never worked too hard on any assignment because she knew there would always be an opportunity to pick up some extra credit later. This is not true in college courses. You need to be serious about coursework, deadlines, and exams from the beginning. Your grade is based on the quality of your work. You need to listen to the cues that the instructor gives about what gets you the grade. And it is not extra credit.

If you are offered a rare opportunity for extra credit, give it your best try. It might help your grade. If it is a tough extra assignment and you try but don't master it, your effort shows your professor that you are a dedicated student.

I confess that I have given extra credit, but very rarely. I have given one or two extra points on a quiz if students attended (on their own time) a lecture by a visiting speaker. Once I offered a challenging problem to two calculus classes. Out of seventy students, only one student turned anything in. He did a good job. He deserved extra credit. Most students want extra credit for doing fluff.

Beware of asking the question, "Will this be on the test?" It suggests your main concern is your grade, while professors consider everything they include in the course to be important and worth learning. Focus on concepts and use your notes to remind you of the big ideas of the class. If you listen carefully to what the professor seems to emphasize, you will have clues about what is likely to be on the next test. However, everything is fair game.

Monitor your grades throughout the semester. Keep your own records of your grades. Keep all graded papers that are returned to you in case any grade needs verification. If your grades are posted on your college's online course software, make sure the scores are entered correctly.

Estimate your own standing rather than email your professor to ask, "What is my grade so far?" or, "What do I have to get on the final to get a B?" The exact average should not affect your study time for future assignments. Just study for everything and attempt to do the best you can on everything. If you feel that your "grade so far" is concerning, go to the professor and discuss it.

> Good grades are *earned*, not given.

If you disagree with the grading, go to see the professor. Make a polite inquiry into the reason for the grade. There may be an error in grading or you may learn more about what to improve upon for the next assignment. If a grader or graduate assistant graded the paper, see her first. If there are still questions you may see the professor, who is the ultimate authority. Do it in a timely fashion instead of waiting until the course is over.

> The grade of A in college is harder to earn than in high school! The grade of B is considered a good grade.

Can you see your final exam once the course is over? You usually will not get your final exam back; however, instructors are usually required by university policy to keep them for some period of time, such as a semester or a year. If you want to see it, go to the instructor soon after the exam. I appreciate the students who come to see what they did wrong so they can learn from their mistakes. It also shows they care about understanding the material.

Exams given earlier in the semester might not be returned, either. All students have the right to see their test results and review them, but they do not have the right to keep the papers if the instructors want to keep them. Some instructors reuse test questions that have worked well for them in the past and do not want the questions being passed on to future students. In some cases, tests are issued by the department to ensure parity between sections. The department may even forbid instructors from returning these tests.

Late assignments. Some professors state in the syllabus that assignments and papers will not be accepted late. You need to plan ahead so you don't get caught at the last minute without time to finish. Other professors may give penalties for late papers. When assignments come in late, they are more difficult to grade. Subjective grading takes a significant amount of time and psychological energy. Conscientious graders may grade in parallel (grade Question 1 on every paper, then Question 2 on every paper, etc.) to ensure consistency in grading. When a paper is graded after the class set, it might require returning to a set of notes about how certain problems were dealt with. The momentum that the grader built up is lost. Your paper may become a "loose end" on the professor's desk or an ignored cell in the grading software. Your paper will get the best consideration if it meets the deadline.

I tend to react to student behaviors in terms of logical extremes. If a student asks if he can turn a paper in late, I multiply this request by the number of students in the course. That would be a disaster! I am pretty firm about "deadlines are deadlines."

There are, however, always exceptions to any rule. If you have a serious problem, go to see the professor in his office to see if you can work something out. Professors are people too, and they recognize when things are out of your control. Waiting too long to start the assignment is *not* one of those exceptions. *Grading is a hard job.* It is the part of teaching that most professors like least. If you meet the deadlines, follow directions, and turn in excellent work, it makes the job easier.

Upper-level students can be hired as graders. I once had a grader (math major) grade a set of homework papers for my first-semester calculus students. She came back saying, "I learned so much from doing this." "Calculus?" I asked. "No . . . about how hard grading is." She said she would never complain about the grading on her own papers again.

Missed exams. It is rare that students miss these important events. Most professors have a policy about whether missed exams may be made up. Read the syllabus to know what it is. "I didn't feel well" will probably not get you a make-up. You will have to provide documentation for the reason you missed the exam so be prepared to go to the health center or the Dean of Students office to verify your excuse.

Can you improve your work and resubmit it? This might be the case in some courses, but it is rare. You need to do your very best on each assignment with the assumption that you get only one chance. If an instructor offers you the opportunity to submit an assignment early for comment, do it by the deadline given.

What is an incomplete grade? From time to time there is an extenuating circumstance that keeps a student from completing an exam or assignment that is required before the final grade is given. An example might include a severe illness or a family emergency that prevents a student from taking the final exam. If the instructor feels that circumstances merit an extension

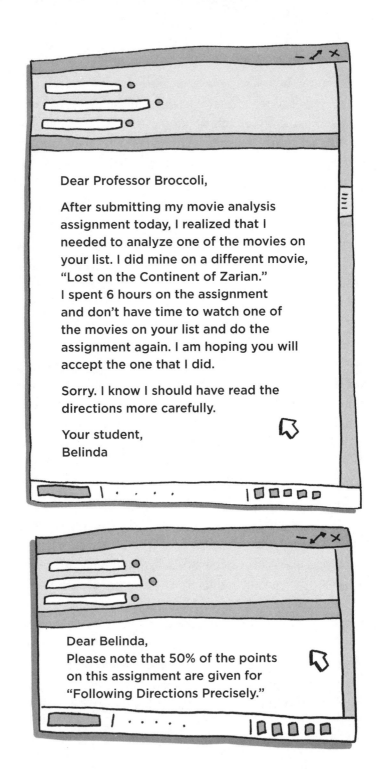

Dear Professor Broccoli,

After submitting my movie analysis assignment today, I realized that I needed to analyze one of the movies on your list. I did mine on a different movie, "Lost on the Continent of Zarian." I spent 6 hours on the assignment and don't have time to watch one of the movies on your list and do the assignment again. I am hoping you will accept the one that I did.

Sorry. I know I should have read the directions more carefully.

Your student,
Belinda

Dear Belinda,
Please note that 50% of the points on this assignment are given for "Following Directions Precisely."

beyond the last day of the semester, he may assign a final grade of "Incomplete." A dean may have to approve this.

If you are granted an incomplete, it is your responsibility to complete the missing work by the deadline given by the instructor. There may not be any reminders. You should complete the work comfortably before the expected deadline. It takes the instructor some time to grade it and initiate the "change of grade" process. At some colleges grades that are not changed to a letter grade by the deadline will automatically become an F, so it is important to pay attention and get the work done!

What is a "participation grade"? Professors often attribute a percentage of the final grade to "participation." This may include attendance (since you can't participate if you are not there), quality of your discussion, and cooperation in group activities. A student may argue that he was sick for the five classes he missed and that these absences should not be counted against him. Unless the professor offers an alternate way to make this up, the student must understand that he will not receive credit for a requirement he did not complete. This includes participation. I know of a course that met once a week for three hours. If you missed a class, you could do a major project to substitute for the class time or you got no credit for participation. The instructor told me that few students ever missed that class!

Transcripts. Once you finish your degree, all you may have is your grades on your transcript. You need to monitor the transcript every semester. It is usually available online. If you feel there is an error, you need to consult the professor immediately, especially if you are near graduation. If you wait, the professor may have retired, have gone on sabbatical leave, or have changed employment without access to the records he needs to answer your inquiry.

Why Should You Care about Grades?

Good grades are an indication that you are able to work hard. An occasional C is fine, but you need to aim higher. There may be scholarships you can apply for if your GPA is high enough. Grades can make a big difference in whether you get the job you want when you graduate. Later, when you establish a reputation in the workplace, your GPA is not as important as your accomplishments on the job.

As an an undergrad, you may not know whether you will apply to grad school or a professional school, so it is best to keep up your grades so your options are not limited. Suppose after working for a few years you see the light on your career path and find it shining toward graduate school. Some programs may require a minimum undergrad GPA of 3.0 (out of 4.0) or even better for consideration. Your grades in your first year of college count as much as those in your last year. If you can avoid digging a big hole in your freshman year, it will help avoid disappointment later.

CHAPTER 12

Polishing Your Written Work

A friend once told me a story about a paper she turned in for a college class. She wrote what she thought was a reasonable paper on the topic, and found that when she had finished, she was half a page short of the required assignment length. She added an extra paragraph of rehashed summary at the end, making the paper exactly the required length. When papers were returned, she was disappointed that she received a grade of D. The professor drew a line above the extra unnecessary material and wrote, "This is fluff. If it wasn't here, your grade would have been a B."

Good Writing Is an Important Skill for College and Beyond

College writing assignments are about much more than simply filling up pages. Learning to write well is a valuable skill that you will need to use in nearly any job requiring a college degree. Scientists write grants and publish their research. Financial analysts and computer programmers write reports and documentation. Almost every job requires emails to your boss and your team. Written communications with clients can be a key to your success. These should be clear and easy for others to understand and free of spelling and grammar mistakes.

There are many books and sources dedicated to writing excellent college analytical and research papers, and you should read those. You may also take a freshman composition course that goes into detail on research techniques, sources, and critical thinking. This chapter, on the other hand, is intended to tell you how to deliver a paper that will meet your professor's overall expectations.

College Papers Can Be Challenging

You will be asked to write many papers in college. Most college papers require some level of analysis, not simply a summary of the literature on a topic. The professor may ask you to take a point of view and support it with evidence from published literature. You may be asked to identify literary techniques and interpret what an author meant in certain words and passages. Some college papers may require references, while others may not. You may be asked to write a "reflection paper" based on assigned readings or a "lab report" describing the results of an experiment you completed in class. In most cases, you will be required to think more critically about a topic than you did in many of your high school courses.

The instructor will give you guidance on what she expects in the way the assignment is presented. Always follow those guidelines—they are crucial for success. There may be a rubric with the grading criteria laying out everything for you. The rubric is your recipe for earning a good grade on the assignment. It tells you what the professor is looking for and exactly what you will be graded upon. Refer to it before you get started, while you are writing, and again when you've finished. Print a copy of the rubric and try "grading" yourself with it. If something required by the rubric is missing or your ideas are not well developed, go back and fix it.

Citing Sources

Most major writing assignments will require you to cite sources. The assignment may specify a minimum number, but in other cases, it is up to students to use their own judgment about how well they have supported their arguments with published citations. A professor may still deduct points for not backing up the arguments with enough published literature, even if a minimum number of citations is not specified in the assignment.

A professor may give the students a guide to formatting references with examples, or he may simply specify a format with a name such as American Psychological Association (APA style), Modern Language Association (MLA style), or *The Chicago Manual of Style*. Always follow the formatting guidelines exactly. Your professor may seem picky for taking points off for using the wrong punctuation in a reference, but if you publish a paper someday, formatting is very important.

In high school you may have written papers that were designed to show you found and organized information and understood a topic. You may have used an encyclopedia, *Wikipedia*, or news articles from publications such as the *New York Times*. In college, for most of your papers your professors will ask you for original analysis, and they will often ask you to rely on "peer-reviewed" sources of information, rather than newspapers, magazines, and books written for the general public. This means that this research is published in scholarly journals or by academic publishers, and that experts in the field have examined the work and think it is worthy of being published. The audience for peer-reviewed publications is other experts in the field. If you are ever unsure whether a publication is peer reviewed, a librarian would be happy to help you.

> Personal web pages and *Wikipedia* are never appropriate resources for a college paper.

Peer-reviewed literature can be described as either "primary" or as a "review paper." The primary literature describes new research. A review paper summarizes the research of others and draws some conclusions from across multiple publications. Many college papers you will write will be similar to these peer-reviewed "review papers." If you are required to use a certain number of sources from the primary literature, it is usually acceptable to include some review papers above and beyond those.

If you cite a textbook in a paper, remember that it is not primary literature.

It is your responsibility to make sure that information you cite in papers comes from reputable sources. Much of the information found on the internet is inaccurate, and it changes frequently. If you cite something, you want a reader to be able to refer to that source and read exactly what you read. Avoid using websites as sources unless your instructor has specifically stated that you may. Even if websites are allowed, only use those that are maintained by reputable organizations. Peer-reviewed papers published in journals that appear only on the internet, like *PLOS*, are fine.

Feedback on Your Work

In most cases, you will turn in only one draft of your paper, so make it a good one. In other cases, you may be required to turn in a rough draft on one date and a final draft at a later date. Treat the rough draft as you would a final draft. Give it your best effort, and turn in the most polished paper that you can. You will probably get some very good feedback on how to make a good paper an excellent one. If the rough draft is graded, you will earn a better grade.

Professors who assign a rough draft and a final draft of the same paper are really trying to help you learn to write well.

Show them that you appreciate the opportunity to improve on your work by using their feedback. It is very frustrating to a professor who has taken the time to write many comments on a paper to see the unedited paper resubmitted.

You may receive comments about the content of your paper, the way that the ideas are presented, or the strength of your arguments to back up the claims made. If you are unsure of how to address a professor's comments, go to his office hours and discuss the paper with him, but do not try to argue your way to a better grade. It will not work. Accept the criticism as a learning opportunity.

Don't expect your professor to make edits for you. She may circle a grammar mistake but not tell you why it is incorrect. It is up to you to figure out what needs to be changed and why. Look for similar errors throughout the paper and try to correct them yourself. You will learn a lot from this process. If you receive a comment involving some sort of grammar lingo, such as "comma splice" or "subject-verb agreement," and you don't know what this means, look it up. Also, don't expect a professor to mark every grammar and spelling mistake. Professors spend a great deal of time grading and cannot comment on every error if there are many.

However, most writing assignments will require only one version of the paper. Even though you will not be revising, it is still important to read every comment the professor has made and to learn from it. Don't assume that the comments are on the front page only. They may be sprinkled throughout the paper, so find them all. If you take them seriously, you may be able to apply some of what you have learned to future classes or even future assignments in the same class.

Be patient in waiting for feedback. Grading papers takes a lot of time. Some professors read the paper briefly and return it with few or no comments, while others write a lot. Waiting longer than you would like to get your paper returned is well worth it for thoughtful feedback. Professors who give the most thoughtful feedback may spend thirty minutes or more per paper.

Getting Additional Help

Your professor. Sometimes students approach professors and ask them to read a draft before the due date, even if it is not required. It is wonderful that these students have started early enough that they can have time to revise their work. However, few professors have the extra time to do this. If your professor says no, don't be offended. Some professors I know will read a draft only if the student arrives in person during office hours, but not if a student emails a draft. Others will read the paper but only if it's in more than a week before the due date.

The campus writing center. If you are struggling with an assignment or simply want to polish your writing skills a bit, a visit to the school's writing center is probably your best option. Most schools offer wonderful writing services free of charge, and the staff are trained in coaching students to write well. Contact the writing center shortly after your paper is assigned and find out how far in advance you need to bring in your paper. You can find out if there are drop-in hours or if an appointment is required. Be sure to tell the staff what kind of class you are writing for at the time you make your appointment. They may have staff members who specialize in the sciences or humanities. The style of writing can be very different for these subjects. Some centers meet with you face-to-face and give feedback on the spot, while others provide feedback electronically a day or more later. Bring a copy of the assignment and any rubrics provided to your appointment.

Friends. You may want to have a friend or relative read over your paper. This is generally a good idea. They can tell you when your arguments don't make sense or suggest areas that need improvement. However, it is not acceptable to have them make changes for you or rewrite a paragraph.

Reference books on writing. There are many books available that address good writing. We don't intend to duplicate those, but it is a good idea to refer to one of them when questions about grammar or writing style come up. If your professor recommends a book, use it.

Deadlines are deadlines!

I don't think he's here. It was due by 5:00, so hopefully he will think I left it on time.

Before You Turn Your Paper In

- Be sure to follow guidelines for font, margins, page numbers, and so on. If you are not told anything different, double-space the paper and use a sans-serif font, such as Arial size 12, with one-inch margins. Professors know the trick of making the margins and font larger to increase the apparent length of the paper and will not tolerate it.
- If you think you've covered the criteria for the assignment well, and your paper is too short, try adding some new ideas and using more references to back up your arguments. Don't pad your work with unnecessary words. Shorter sentences are usually clearer and easier to read.
- If your paper is too long, first see if you can eliminate unnecessary words to make some sentences smoother and shorter. When citing sources, state what you want to say and then cite. Extra clauses, such as "In a research study, the authors found," are unnecessary. For example,

Avoid this wording	Instead, try this wording
In a research study, the authors found that students who did not use mobile phones in class had better recall of information and a better grade (Kuznekoff, Munz, and Titsworth 2015).	Students who did not use mobile phones in class had better recall of information and a better grade (Kuznekoff, Munz, and Titsworth 2015).

- Still too long? Decide what the most important points are and cut less important material. You will not get extra credit for producing a longer product than requested. Some professors take off points for papers that are too long. Learning to write with space constraints is important, as you may encounter these requirements on the job.

- Proofread the paper. This applies to everything you write from a term paper to a homework response. Poor grammar and spelling not only make your work hard to read, but can also change the meaning of your intended point entirely. Reading your

  Proofread everything you write!

  paper aloud to yourself is also a good idea. If a sentence doesn't read smoothly when you say it, revise it until it is clear and concise.
- Pay special attention to the formatting of scientific names, chemical formulas, and equations. This is part of demonstrating your scientific and/or mathematical knowledge, and it should be included in your grade.
- If your paper includes figures, graphs, or pictures, double-check the formatting guidelines for labeling and citing these. Make sure that graph axes are clearly labeled with the units and use a font large enough to be easily read.
- Check to see that all references cited in the text are also listed as references at the end and vice versa.
- When you are finished, check for formatting consistency across all pages.
- If you are turning in a hard copy, make sure it is a good one. A blurry paper that gets turned in with a note saying, "Sorry. My printer is running out of ink," is not acceptable. Find another printer or change the ink cartridge.

Turning It In

- Submit electronic copies in the format specified by the professor, such as pdf or Microsoft Word. Other formats may not be compatible with the learning management system. You should combine all parts of the assignment into one document.
- Check your file to make sure you are submitting the correct one, and not an earlier draft, before you submit it. Once the paper is uploaded, click the file to open it and check that the formatting has been preserved. If there are changes, consider resubmitting with a pdf or other file format from the list of acceptable formats.
- Never email a copy of a paper to your professor, unless he has asked you to. The professor wants either a stack of hard copies or a single location in the course's electronic grade book where he can find all student papers together.
- When the instructor asks for a hard copy, it must be a hard copy that you deliver in person by the deadline. You should not expect your professor to print out your paper from an email attachment. If it has multiple pages, staple them.
- Your paper is creative work that needs to make a good impression. If it is a hard copy, keep it safe from coffee spills and crumpling at the bottom of your backpack.

A colleague told me that she asks for hard copies of student papers, but with an electronic backup. Once a student claimed he turned in a paper to her department mailbox, but it was not there. Another claimed to have put a paper under the professor's office door, but it turned out that she got the wrong office. But once the professor started requiring an electronic copy submitted to the learning management system as a backup, the excuses stopped. Timeliness was determined by the time stamp of the electronic submission. She then had copies if she needed to review them while writing a letter of recommendation for a student.

Homework Papers

Since homework problems may be assigned frequently, you may not feel the need to put forth a very polished piece of work. However, your submission needs to be easy for an instructor to read and grade. Generally, if the homework requires any calculations or the drawing of diagrams, it will be easier to turn in handwritten work.

> I could not read your handwriting. You'll have to re-do it if you want credit.

> Sorry. I'm a pre-med student. I'm practicing my handwriting to get into medical school!

Guidelines for Turning In a Handwritten Assignment

- Your handwriting must be legible and neat. Otherwise consider typing it.
- Use blue or black pen. Pencil works well for math or science work. Be sure to erase cleanly. A paper with work crossed out is hard to follow and does not make a good impression.
- If you start a solution and then you start again with a new approach, neatly cross out the wrong one. Better yet, rewrite the page.
- Use paper that does not have fringe hanging off the side from being torn from a spiral notebook.
- Use only one side of the paper if the writing shows through.
- Leave ample margins for the grader to write comments.
- In solutions to math or science problems, a logical train of thought must move from the top of the page to the bottom. Underline or circle your final answer at the end of your work. Recheck the question to see that you have answered what was asked.
- Put your full name, course, and assignment name on the front page. Staple multiple pages.

The most important thing to remember when working on a paper is to start early so you have time to get help and revise multiple times. A little care can go a long way in making your paper a piece of work you will be proud of and your professor will appreciate.

CHAPTER 13

Managing Your Coursework and Your Time

I once had a student who was chronically absent or late to class. His excuse was oversleeping. He set an alarm but he kept hitting "snooze" and not fully waking up. Finally, he solved the problem by writing a program for his computer to set off an alarm that could only be turned off by crossing the room and correctly typing in the answers to some questions that appeared on the screen. I was pleased that it worked. I only wish he had shared the program with all of the other sleepy students at the university.

There are a number of problems that students experience that can get in the way of academic success. These are common ones along with my advice for dealing with them.

Common Challenges That Students Encounter

Missing class. Besides oversleeping, you might miss class for other reasons. You don't show up one day and nothing happens. The professor does not call your parents and she does not embarrass you by asking, "Where were you on Monday?" This makes it easier to do it again, especially if attendance is not required. You rationalize it by saying the class is boring and you can just read the textbook to pass the next quiz. It might work in the short term, but it eventually works against you. In most cases, it takes much more time and effort to learn the material on your own than the time spent in class. Would you buy concert

In September the deadline for this English paper seemed far away. Now it's the end of October and I'm swamped with work for other classes too. I'm going to have to cut my physics class to work on it today.

I'm cutting my English class to work on my physics project!

tickets and not show up for the concert? You are could be wasting even more money by not attending class.

Attending class consistently should be your highest priority. Reserve your absences for emergencies such as illness. If you fumble early in the semester and later regret it, go to see the instructor and repent. Show you are interested in doing better and then do better. Schedule your bedtime so that you can get enough sleep to fully wake up for daylight hours. Chronically missing class is a pattern that can carry over to your post-college life. It will not get you far in the working world.

Procrastination. Work in college courses should be continuous but students tend to treat it as a series of discrete tasks. They put off many assignments until the deadline is near. Procrastination often causes students to ask for extensions or last-minute help. Those requests are not usually fulfilled. I cannot stress enough the importance of starting early on papers and studying throughout the semester. More lead time will allow you to ask for advice or help if you need it and will help generate a better product. If unexpected issues arise, working ahead may keep you out of trouble.

Time management. In high school, your time is highly structured for you. College can be less structured in comparison. Here are some suggestions to help you make the most of your time.

- Daily and weekly planning. You should be spending at least two hours out of class for every hour in class. If you are a full-time student spending fifteen hours in class each week, you should spend at least thirty hours studying and completing assignments. This can be a lot of time to organize on your own. A former student of mine told me that she had a class on Thursdays at 8 a.m. with her only other class that day at 3:00 p.m. She had a hard time using the hours in between efficiently. Eventually she learned to schedule herself into the library and assigned herself blocks of concentrated study time for specific courses.
- Daily study can ward off problems later. Review your notes for each class before the next class. To use a music analogy, should you practice 15 minutes a day or 1.75 hours once a week? What if you waited until the week of the annual recital to do all your practicing?
- The first few weeks of a course may not seem strenuous as there are few deadlines. Then all of a sudden it seems that every class has a midterm during the same week! Daily studying from the beginning can put you in a better position to make it through this stressful week.

- Arrange study time to work in small, efficient chunks. Take breaks to allow yourself to regroup.
- If you work with a classmate, make appointments to study together. Procrastination is harder when someone else is depending on you to contribute to a group.
- Plan for the long term. Because there are not many incremental deadlines for college assignments, deadlines may seem very far off. Any distraction can derail you from making progress. We all do better with deadlines. Learning to set intermediate deadlines for yourself can make a big difference. Write them on your calendar instead of just thinking you can always start that paper tomorrow instead of today.

> Procrastination and lack of sleep are two of the most common problems for college students. Schedule both your work and your sleep to avoid problems.

Managing Your Coursework

Is this class the right one for you? Sometimes you will find yourself in a course that you are not prepared for or that is not what you thought it would be. You need to figure this out before the drop/add period ends so you can change your schedule. If you are unsure of whether you belong, go to see the professor as soon as possible to sort it out.

Make friends with some juniors and seniors. They can be good mentors. Ask them what their favorite courses and professors are. This can help you make good choices.

Not registered for the course you want? Go anyway on the first day. A lot of important information is given then. You can hope for a seat to open up for you to register or you might be able to get on a waiting list. But maybe you will decide that it is not the class for you anyway. If a course you really want is full, linger after class or go to the office of the professor and ask if it is possible to be put on a waiting list or get an override, which is special permission to register. Be aware that if you get the override, the professor has done you a favor and you need to return the favor by attending class regularly and showing interest in the course.

Course load feels too heavy. If you are in a course that you feel you are not ready for, drop it early. Mark the deadline for drop/add on your calendar and do your soul-searching before that date. For some period after that you may be able to "withdraw," but it may be permanently recorded on your transcript as a withdrawal and you don't get your tuition back. It will also be too late to substitute a different course. Meet with your advisor to get some input.

Be careful about choosing an ambitious course schedule for your first semester. If you are overwhelmed by the workload, you might be better off taking only twelve credit hours for one semester. You can't do that every semester unless you want to spend more time, money, and opportunity cost in school, but it is better to do this for one semester than to fail some classes. If you are short on credits you might take a course or two in summer school to catch up.

If you are worried about feeling comfortable in the classes you choose, you might register for one more course than you need with the intention of dropping your least favorite class before the deadline.

Grades need improvement. This book is full of suggestions that can help you improve grades and optimize your performance. However, until you hard-wire those things into your college routine, you may feel your grades need boosting. If so, make a visit to your professor and see if he can help you analyze your progress so far and your weak spots and make suggestions. You should go seeking advice, not extra-credit opportunities, extensions, or redos.

A poor grade early in the course does not mean you are going to fail. Each new assignment, quiz, test, lab, project, or presentation is a new opportunity to dilute the effect of your fumble. Shake off your discouragement and plunge ahead!

College can be more challenging than high school. Maybe everything was easy for you in high school, but you may find that some of your college courses are more rigorous or your preparation is lacking. Some common student comments are:

- There is not a lot of time in class to ask questions.
- The class feels rushed.
- I wish we could have seen more problems worked out in class.
- There was so much material covered in such a short time.

These comments do not mean there is something wrong with these students or with their professors. It is normal for college courses to feel fast and furious. You will need to adjust your strategies to meet the new demands, rather than blame the system or someone else as the cause for your discomfort. (That is what this book is about.)

Managing exams. Students often think of every exam as a monumental hurdle. This may be because they are not studying regularly and reviewing in smaller chunks along the way. Each exam is only one piece of the grade puzzle. There are often many smaller pieces that are easier to excel in, such as homework, papers, or class participation. Make sure you attend to those pieces to cushion your grade against a less favorable exam outcome. Avoid thinking that poor performance on one test will doom you. Adding to your anxiety will not help.

How to maximize your study time for a test:

- If the professor has an optional review session, be sure to go. Do some preparation beforehand and bring questions with you. If the instructor has posted practice problems or a test from a previous year, complete these ahead of time.
- Avoid a distracting environment—not a busy coffee shop or the dorm. If you find a favorite place to study, such as a quiet table in a library, you can train your brain to associate that place with concentrating on studying.
- The night before the test, review the toughest topics again right before you go to sleep.
- Don't set your alarm to wake up early to study as it might disrupt your REM sleep.
- Don't pull an all-nighter to study. Your brain will not recover from the lack of sleep in time to do well on the test.
- Do not skip breakfast. Eat oatmeal or some other high-carb, high-fiber food.
- Students tend to focus on facts rather than concepts while studying. Avoid rote memorization. Be able to *explain* the concepts of the course. If you work with a study group, you can help each other by talking about clarifying content and concepts.
- Before an exam, your group can write a practice test, take it, and discuss your answers. This is great test preparation as you can't write the test unless you can identify the major ideas of the course.

Exam anxiety. Getting too worked up about taking an exam is usually detrimental to performance. By preparing in both the short term and long term you will feel less anxious. Then try

your best. If the exam is in an unfamiliar room, visit it early to see where you would like to sit for best conditions—the lighting is good, you can see the clock (you may not be able to use your phone to check the time), and not near the door where you could be bothered by latecomers and early leavers. If the room is available for studying, try sitting in your favorite seat. If you write a practice test with your study group, take it there.

Not enough time on exams? Students often complain that they would have done better on an exam if they had more time. This might be a shock to students who had exams in high school that were easy to finish quickly or where teachers gave extra time to anyone who wanted it. This is not the case in college courses. When you take an exam, you are being given a chance to show what you can do in a specific amount of time. This is a critical part of demonstrating that you really know the material. You are compared to what others in your class can do in the same amount of time. One of my colleagues calls the day of an exam "Opportunity Day"—it is your opportunity to show what you know.

It takes some skill to decide where your precious time pays off the most during an exam. Lingering on each question in order may not be your best strategy. If you move ahead to look for questions you can answer quickly and accurately, you may lessen your anxiety, increase your confidence, and maximize your score.

Test prep may be similar to prepping for a race or learning your lines for a play. Practice is important to get you fluid with the content and speed. You need to study consistently throughout the course, not just cram for exams. Your future boss will expect you to work hard throughout a project, not just push at the end and then complain that you could have done better if you had more time.

Getting Help

Feeling overwhelmed emotionally or academically? Establishing good communication early with your professors can pay off. When you have a serious issue that affects your class work, see the professor. Save your requests for the important stuff, however. No matter how many times the professor says, "Absolutely no extensions!" there are circumstances outside of your control that warrant exceptions.

If your issue affects all your classes or you are too overwhelmed to talk to your professor, contact the Dean of Students office. These are people who are equipped to help you figure out what to do. It may be a death in the family, depression, bad choices on your part, or unforeseen life events. University staff can intervene on your behalf with your professors to develop a plan to help you. They can help you make an appointment with the counseling center too.

Other campus resources. Learn about what is available on your campus. When you start to have problems, use these resources. Common ones include:

- Your faculty advisor. Most students only use this person for advice on courses and meeting requirements for a major, but you can get some good academic guidance if you need someone to talk to.
- Department chair. If you have a problem with a professor that you need help with, go to the chair of the department.
- Health center or counseling center. Your physical and mental health affect your academic performance so don't wait too long to get help with any problems you are experiencing.
- Writing center. Writing papers can be a huge hurdle so schedule some advice to get you going or improve your paper.
- Tutoring or academic resource center. Names for these vary, but most colleges have somewhere that students can go to learn study skills, attend seminars on important skills such as note-taking, and meet with a free tutor for some subjects.

- Private tutors. Often the departments keep a list of tutors for their discipline.
- Reference desk at the library. One of my librarian friends says that students do not understand how much reference librarians enjoy helping students and faculty. Yes, even the faculty ask them questions.

Conclusion

Here is a summary list of some key strategies that may help you avoid or solve problems.

1. Get more sleep. Schedule it. Keeping the same bedtime each day can really help.
2. Start early on assignments so you meet the deadlines comfortably.
3. Study every day, not just at test time.
4. Schedule your own intermediate deadlines so you don't fall prey to procrastination. Write them on a calendar.
5. Attend all classes. Stay undistracted and focused.
6. Go to see the professor early. Go again when there are problems.
7. Don't be afraid to ask questions, early and often.
8. Meet students in every one of your classes and become a support group, study group, safety net, and sounding board for each other.

I assure you that everyone has some problems while in college. With good planning, you will be prepared to overcome them quickly or find help when needed. Every course is a new beginning. If you play sports you know that each new game is like that. Don't assume that your stumble in the past will handicap you in the future. Learn from your mistakes and use that knowledge to be a winner in the next course. As you progress through college, you will figure out what works best for you. Don't worry if you struggle the first semester—everyone else is in the same boat.

CHAPTER 14

Ethical Considerations

I was enjoying the roar of the ocean on a beach in Florida over spring break. It was a popular destination for college students. A small propeller plane flew offshore with a banner trailing behind that read, "Essay due? EduPaper will write it for you!" I felt like a judge might feel if the banner read, "Speeding ticket? We can fix it for you!"

My sister turned to me and said, "Isn't that illegal? How can they do this?" I don't believe it's illegal to write college papers for someone else. But it is definitely unethical. And if you turn in a paper you didn't write yourself, you will be in big trouble with your college.

Ways Students Are Not Honest and How They Might Be Noticed

Professors view all student work and student behaviors with a great deal of professional scrutiny. They are less interested in catching a cheater than in keeping everyone honest. It is extremely distressing and personally offensive to an instructor to detect dishonesty on the part of a student. Professors are very familiar with ways in which students might not be honest and are good at spotting them. Here are some common infractions and ways professors prevent or discover them.

Plagiarism. You may not copy any part of the work of others. You may not submit a paper, or any part of one, that you wrote for another course. You must cite your sources for everything.

Many colleges have a service such as turnitin.com that scans your paper for plagiarism concerns. The program compares it to everything available on the internet as well as papers previously turned in from college courses. Since many assignments are now turned in electronically, it is easier than ever to detect dishonesty. It may also be considered plagiarism if you do not cite sources correctly.

Ghostwriting in which someone else writes your paper for you. Usually ghostwriting is done through an online service, but having another student write a paper for you is also unethical. Papers that are better than the past performance of a student are often a flag for this. Electronic plagiarism checkers are often able to spot these papers.

Using an online translator for your foreign-language home-work. These translators have a style that is easy for professors to notice, so they will figure out that you have used it.

Cheating on an exam. Instructors may use more than one form of an exam or seat students in different seating patterns during an exam to thwart copying. You may be asked to cover your work with a cover sheet. It is only fair to honest students to provide comfortable testing conditions that are free of distractions. Instructors may require students to leave their phones and notebooks in their backpacks and place them at the front of the room. Even having a phone or notebook in sight may be considered a violation of the honor code.

Lying about excuses. Claims of illness may require a note from a doctor or the college health center. Those notes can be checked and often are. A student once emailed me to say he would not be in class because his grandmother died. I notified the Dean of Students office. They called the parents to verify and found it was not true. Checking on documentation is not intended to be distrustful. It is a policy that needs to be consistent. If not, students may take advantage.

Some instructors require any students who miss an exam to contact the Dean of Students office to explain their situation and get a note. It's a pain for professors to verify the student's story. Also, working with the dean can be helpful to the student. If a student has missed multiple classes and needs to work things out with several professors, she needs to explain her situation to only one person, and a letter from the dean is readily accepted by faculty.

When an excuse seems flimsy, instructors often ask questions of students and the excuses fall apart. A student once said she had to miss class because she "had to see someone about a job." When I probed a bit, I found that she was seeing someone about entering a pageant. I suggested that the pageant appointment could be rescheduled but my class could not.

Working together on an assignment when it is not allowed. Often students are told they must work alone. But when two of them submit work that has an identical solution, paragraph, or unusual idea, the instructor might uncover cooperation by interviewing the students separately. It usually reveals the truth, one way or another.

Sending someone else to take an exam in your place. In large lecture classes where the instructor does not know every student by sight, it is common to require an ID to enter the exam room. Often graduate students are enlisted to help monitor exams.

Missing an exam so the student can find out from another student what is on the exam. Often a make-up exam, however, is not the same exam that was taken by the rest of the class. I know one professor who gives oral exams in the case of a make-up— you have to go to his office and explain the answers out loud. Not many students want to do this so they make every effort to attend the scheduled exam.

Claiming work was turned in when it was not. This is usually an excuse for not doing the work. If the instructor probes to find out exactly how the work was turned in, there is usually some departure from the directions given about submittal.

> Take an honest approach to all your college work. If you can't do it without cheating, you should not be there.

Changing answers on a returned paper and then complaining that something was marked wrong when it seems to be right. When professors are concerned about this, they scan the papers before returning them. Then looking for student changes after papers are graded and returned is easy.

We had a flat tire on the way to the exam! Sorry we missed it.
Here is the make-up exam. There is only one question.
NAME
DATE
1 WHICH TIRE WAS FLAT?

Dishonesty Affects Everyone

Once a student pulls off a case of cheating (even suspected cheating), it makes the instructor more suspicious of everyone. For example, if a student is craning his neck to see the paper next to him, the instructor might insist on cover sheets for everyone.

I once had a student who did not turn in a midterm exam paper. He was there, but he knew he failed the test so he just kept the paper and slipped out of the room with the paper under his jacket. He wanted me to think that I was the one who had lost the paper. It was hard to prove, so I did not turn him in for cheating. I offered him a make-up test, but he never showed up to take it. I was traumatized by this event and decided I would never let it happen again. So, I started checking off student names as they turned in their papers and matched them against who was there. I doubt that any of my other students ever thought of such a scheme, but I felt I had to protect myself from a charge that I lost the paper. Believe me, I treat my papers as if they were gold!

What Happens to Students Who Are Found to Be Unethical?

The academic world is very sensitive to dishonesty. Academic work is considered the pursuit of truth. That is why honor codes are common on college campuses. Depending on how the honor code is structured, violations may be handled by the instructor, by a dean, or by an honor council. Even if there is not a formal honor code, there are consequences for cheating.

Suppose a student turns in a lab report that meets the requirements of the assignment given except that it describes a procedure from last year's lab that was changed in this year's assignment. It is obviously copied from last year. What happens to the student? There is a wide range of possibilities from a grade of zero on the assignment or an F for the course to being suspended from school for the semester without a refund. It could be difficult to explain to a prospective employer why you were not in school for a semester.

If your college has an honor code, you will be introduced to it during your orientation. You may have to sign your work to say that it meets the requirements of the honor code. If an incident is reported to an honor council, there is an investigation, a trial, and a sentence if you are found guilty. It is not a process you want to experience firsthand. Dishonesty jeopardizes everything about the mission of academic institutions so they take it very seriously.

Ethical Behavior Extends to All That You Do in College

If you have work-study employment, you need to show up at your scheduled times and do a good job. If a professor hires you to help with her research project, you must take it seriously and never cut corners. If you are hired to tally the number of times a bird pecks on an apple, you need to do it accurately. If you just write something down so you can go home and take a nap, you are guilty of a severe breach of scientific protocol. This would not just anger the professor, it might cause you to be sent to the honor council, and you might be kicked out of school.

I once had a student who said she could not take a midterm because her teenaged brother had been in a motorcycle accident and she had to go home. I was upset by the vision of a near-death scene in a hospital emergency room. I sympathetically agreed and sent her along with best wishes for her family.

Upon her return, I inquired about her brother and discovered the story to be somewhat different from the one she presented earlier. It turns out that he was never in a hospital. Her stepmother had asked my student to babysit a younger child so she could take her teenager to a follow-up doctor appointment. I would not have agreed to the delayed test if I had understood the circumstances to be what they were. I would have asked the student to take the test before she left or ask the stepmother to make other babysitting arrangements.

This story isn't one about what we think of as cheating, but it does illustrate some erosion in my trust of this student. In fact, there were more excuses offered by her throughout the semester for late work, poor work, or requests for extensions. I did not take them seriously because of my first experience. I have found that students who are willing to stretch the truth once do it routinely. A pattern like this can derail your degree and your career plans.

Why did this student behave in these ways? I think she did not put her college courses as a high priority in her life so she succumbed to other competing distractions. Then when she wanted to avoid negative consequences from me, she resorted to fibs and cutting corners.

Why Do Students Cheat?

Most students do not plan on cheating. They have good intentions but things go wrong and they take what they think is the easy way out. The top two reasons students cheat are (1) they are not doing well in the course and are desperate to bring up the grade, and (2) they did not leave enough time to complete the assignment or study for the test. They rationalize their dishonesty by saying everybody else does it. But they don't.

Dear Professor Broccoli,

How many words do I have to change in a sentence so it is not considered plagiarized?

Thanks,
Sam

Some students are lazy and fall into the easiest way to accomplish an assignment or get a reasonable grade without doing the work themselves. This usually becomes apparent and when it is discovered, the student's educational career can be compromised.

How to Avoid the Appearance of Dishonesty

Professors have years of practice in knowing what to expect from students and noticing suspicious variations. Honest students may be offended by controls for cheating. But in the end, their work is protected by efforts to thwart unethical behavior.

If you are an honest student, you don't want anyone to suspect you of anything less. You can take precautions to avoid the appearance of dishonesty because the process for sorting it out is not easy or pleasant. Here are some suggestions:

- When you take a test, don't sit next to the person you studied with. If you both mis-studied something and write the same unusual response or solution, you cannot be accused of collaborating during the exam.
- If you bring notes to study in the few minutes before an exam, make sure they are zipped in your backpack before the exam is passed out. Don't just stash your open notebook under the desk.
- If you need scrap paper during an exam, ask the instructor or proctor for some. If you use your own, someone may think you are bringing notes in on the paper.
- Use a cover sheet during a paper/pencil exam so that it does not appear that you are allowing others to read from your paper. Ask the proctor for one.
- Read the requirements for every exam carefully. If you miss a special statement such as "no calculators," it is not an excuse for using one.
- Become very familiar with the requirements for every assignment. If you are not sure what resources are allowed, ask first. If the directions say you must complete the work without help from anyone else, not knowing will not excuse you from violating the rules.
- If you do homework with another student, it may be fine to discuss it. But write up your own understandings or problem solutions.
- If you copy and paste text from the internet or other electronic source with the intention of summarizing or quoting from it later, be sure to label it so you know it is not your own words. It is best to store it in a resource file, not the file

with the actual paper you are writing. It is easy to lose track of what you wrote yourself and what you didn't. Changing a few words or patching sentences from multiple sources does not make it original work.

- Keep a copy of every paper, problem set, or project that you turn in so that if the grader says he does not have it, you can replace it.
- If you have access to graded work from previous semesters from a friend or a fraternity file, don't fall into the trap of looking at it. Professors often change something that will tip them off when they see something in your work that was part of an old assignment but not the current one. Doing your own work is the best safeguard!
- Be careful about sharing your old homework, labs, and papers with your friends. They may just want an example of how the assignment could be completed, but if your work ends up being copied, you may be in trouble for assisting them.
- Plan ahead. Start early. Don't set your standards so high that you feel forced to cheat to attain the grade you planned to achieve.

Trust Is Essential to Relationships in College and Your Post-College Life

While you are in college it is important to develop a trusting relationship with your professors. Dishonesty destroys that trust. Your good reputation is precious so don't do anything to hurt it.

There are many well-publicized cases of people in the working world who have failed to meet ethical standards and have suffered greatly as a result. Among them are journalists who made up events that they reported as true; people who claimed to have college degrees they don't have; politicians, elected officials, authors, songwriters, religious leaders who lifted some of their material from the work of others; people who stole money from their employer; and people who went to prison for lying when under investigation. The best way to avoid being caught in dishonesty is to be honest—in your coursework, in your career, and in your personal life!

PART V

FINAL WORDS OF WISDOM

CHAPTER 15

For Parents

Preparing, Supporting, and Understanding Your Student

I returned to my office after my 9 a.m. calculus class. The office phone rang, and it was the father of one of the students in the class I had just left. He was worried because he had been trying to call his son since the prior evening and he was not answering his cell phone. "Was he in class this morning?" he asked anxiously.

Wow! How did he know his schedule and that I was the instructor?

I knew the son was in class (he always sat in the middle of the front row) and that he was his usual animated self. I said to the father, "I believe that your son is over eighteen. Therefore, I am very sorry to say that unless I have signed permission from him, I can't tell you anything about him. But I will tell you that, in general, students like to think of themselves as independent when they go away to college so he may not share your perspective of wanting him to check in frequently. Or his cell phone wasn't charged. At any rate, I am sure you will hear from him soon."

For many families, the beginning of college is the first time parents and students have been separated for long stretches of time. This can be hard, especially when parents are used to knowing about their child's daily activities and academic progress. In high school parents may have been able to log onto a school record-keeping site to review all their child's progress. Colleges usually do not send grades to parents unless the student signs permission for the registrar to send a copy to the parents.

I have two daughters who went away to college. I know how hard it is to let go. In close families, it can feel like bereavement. I know the feeling of "they grow so fast!" I was thinking about it recently when I held my granddaughter's hand as I walked her to preschool. You want to hold that hand forever, but the best thing you can do is to teach your children to function without you so that when they do go to college (and ultimately work), they can manage without everyday supports from you.

Start Preparing Your Child Well in Advance of College

Every parent wishes for their children to become emotionally and financially independent. Here are some ideas for setting the stage early that might pay off for you and your child.

Create a sense of independence and responsibility early. Have your kids set their own alarm clocks, pack their own lunches, keep their own calendars, pay some of their own expenses, and do their own schoolwork beginning in elementary school. Let them take responsibility for deadlines, decisions, and the quality of their work. It may be better for them to experience a stumble or failure while they are living with you than to be far from home when the first catastrophe occurs. You can empower your kids to recover from their own mistakes.

Create a positive view of college as a time for personal and intellectual growth. If you attended college, mention your academic successes. Even if you didn't have many, you might say something such as, "I wish I had worked harder in Spanish class because it would have paid off in the job I have now." Or, "I wish I had taken more business courses." My mother once told me a story about enjoying a trigonometry class in college. If she had said, "I've never been very good at math," it may have affected my own confidence in my choice of major.

If you made good friends or business connections in college, weave that into conversations with your kids. It shows that there are lifelong relationships to be gained.

If you did not attend college, it is never too late to take courses. I love having older students in my classes—I have found them to be more focused, appreciative, and goal oriented. There are many career paths that do not require a college degree, but helping your children be open to the possibility of continuing education after high school may pay off for them.

Encourage work experience before going to college. Part-time jobs in high school, such as mowing lawns, babysitting, waiting tables, or clerking in a store, give students a glimpse into the working world. Dealing with a supervisor, coworkers, and the public can be informative in terms of career choices and educational path. High schools may provide opportunities for mentorships that provide insights into possible career interests. When students read the introduction of this book, they should know the answer to the question, "Why are you going to college?"

Help your children learn the value of dealing with people, not just Google. They may be used to doing everything electronically and may not be comfortable looking people in the eye to ask for help, or calling on the phone. When they experience a demanding, non-nurturing teacher in high school, help them to find a way to thrive in the course despite any personality clashes. There will be some college professors who are tough, but dropping the course may not be the best way to handle the situation.

Help them to be alert to their surroundings and the people around them. College campuses are filled with students who walk around with earbuds in their ears and their heads down, mostly looking at their cell phones. Even when they reach a street, they plunge ahead without looking up. Meeting new people is a skill worth developing. Networking is a lifelong pursuit.

Decisions to Make by the End of High School

Have an early discussion of expectations about college finances. Make the financial arrangements clear. Who is paying for what and for how long? What you decide may influence the choice of college so early discussion is a good idea. If loans are needed, who will sign for them and bear the responsibility of paying them back? How much is your child willing to invest in this preparation? Students who have skin in the game financially may be more serious about making progress.

> Good communication about your expectations and those of your child can be very helpful in making college a successful experience.

My friend, Dave, was a history major in college. He failed an English class his last semester. He had assumed that his professor would pass him despite poor attendance and missing some assignments and an exam. After all, he couldn't graduate without this course. What professor would deny him a degree? When he got the bad news he called his father who said, "We love you," followed by "Remember our agreement about our financial support? It ends this semester." Dave retook the course in summer school. During his search for a way to pay for it, he stumbled into information on financial planning, which eventually led to a career as a certified financial planner. Sometimes a little "sink or swim" pays dividends.

Have a discussion about academic expectations in college. If you communicate healthy expectations of good effort rather than perfect grades, it may lessen the emotional anxiety of some students who are worried about disappointing their parents. Yes, we all want our children to live up to their potential, but if things don't go well, we want to be the support rather than the critic. I have had students come to my office crying over disappointing grades. Sometimes it is pressure from parents that causes the tears. Other times it is disappointment caused by their own perfectionism. I try to encourage them to do their best, but to recognize that As are not the only goal.

Community college may be a good place to start. If your child needs more support or is unsure of whether college is the right path, encourage enrolling in a community college near you to test the waters and learn the ropes. Maybe part-time work and taking a few courses would be a good start. If finances are an issue, living at home while taking courses can save money.

Be open to the idea of a "gap year" or other delay in entering college. Just because everyone else is going to college is not a sufficient reason to enroll. It should be an opportunity rather than a default.

Some students are more successful in college after a year of working or other experience. Researcher Bob Clagett found that students at the University of North Carolina–Chapel Hill and Middlebury College who took a gap year achieved higher GPAs than those who entered college directly from high school. Working or volunteering at a hospital, school, or legal clinic can be helpful in choosing a career path. Living abroad to study or work can be a maturing experience. Colleges are agreeable to having students defer the start of their college work for this gap year.

A friend told me he would have flunked out of college if he had enrolled directly from high school. Instead he spent five years in blue-collar jobs until he was ready for college. Then he graduated with a 4.0 grade point average and went on for a doctorate. He said what he learned in the working world helped him understand himself and set his educational goals. He is now a professor at a large state university. This is the kind of knowledge that is infinitely valuable before you start college.

If finances are an issue, it might be wise to work for a while to save some money before enrolling in courses. Working too many hours a week while taking college courses can backfire. I once had a student who worked three part-time jobs while enrolled as a full-time college student. He could not keep up with his classes and ended up dropping out of school.

When Your Child Enters College

Once your child has committed to college courses, respect the class schedule. Don't plan family trips that require cutting classes or rescheduling exams to go along. If your student lives at home or near you, be careful about leaning too heavily on her to do things for you that interfere with classes. Avoid calling and texting during the times classes are likely to meet.

Be available for support if needed. Your child is an adult once he graduates from high school. It is time to trust him to make his own decisions and mistakes. If he goes away to college, make it clear that you are happy to hear from him and that he should alert you if problems arise. Good communication is key. If you talk through problems, you can help him find the right solutions or people to help him on campus. Your wisdom can be invaluable.

Avoid hovering. You are lucky to have cell phones, text messaging, and emails to facilitate easy communication. Technology can keep students connected to their familiar friends and family, but they need to cultivate relationships in their new surroundings, too. Constant communication from you can be a hindrance to developing emotional independence and problem-solving skills. Students need to meet their own deadlines instead of depending on your constant reminders.

You can encourage your child to take the lead in being in touch so he doesn't feel you are being too hovering. I know parents who limit their calls to once a week. It lets the kids

be independent, but it is enough to let them know you care about them.

If you are really concerned about your child's health, safety, or poor academic performance, call the Dean of Students office and share your concerns. The staff there has procedures in place to check on students when parents or professors alert them to problems.

Parents, when you come to campus to visit your student, don't hesitate to come by the offices of your child's favorite professors. We love meeting parents.

Thank you, parents, for launching your kids and sending them to college. You have made many sacrifices to get them this far. College is an important stage in their life and you deserve credit for getting them there.

CHAPTER 16

Summing Up

College is a wonderful experience if you are prepared, aware, and sensible. We hope this book has helped. When you are ready, go and embrace learning. Be committed to success. Rather than thinking of yourself as a customer who is paying for a degree, consider college your opportunity to reach a goal that will reward you.

A new beginning. Your college education is not an extension of high school but the start of a new phase in your life, a professional one. Whatever your record or reputation was in high school, it is behind you. No one knows what you did or didn't do then. This is a fresh start and you set your own expectations.

You may have noticed some common themes in this book.

- Expect to be treated like an adult in college. Take that seriously and act like one.
- Be prepared and actively engaged in your classes.
- Get to know your professors and aim to impress them with your work.
- In the immortal words of my student, Tyler, in chapter 2, "Go to all your classes and do all the homework!"

Acknowledge those who helped you along the way. This book has been an attempt at letting you see the perspective of your instructors. If you appreciate what any professors have done, tell them. An email is fine. A handwritten note is special.

It is a nice gesture to drop by office hours to see a professor sometime after you finish the course, maybe a year later, to just

report on how things are going. Professors really do care about you. They are happy to hear from you, especially if you have good news to share (you did well in the next course, you are graduating, you have a job lined up, you got into grad school, you had a great experience in your study-abroad program, etc.). Drop by when you come back to campus after graduation or send an email to say that you got promoted.

If things go well, you will build many relationships with your fellow students that will enrich your college years and the years beyond. Networking is the name of the game and your college friends will be part of those connections. When your class reunion events roll around over the years, I hope that you will have many friends that you look forward to seeing again.

If you treat your college years as preparation for the future, the transition to the next stage will be easier. Following our advice, you will come to appreciate your boss, your commanding officer, or your thesis adviser the way you have come to understand your professors.

When you finish college, be sure to thank anyone who provided some financial support. It might be your parents, grandparents, your employer, the military, or a scholarship sponsor. Tell them you are grateful they invested in you. If you paid your own way, you deserve an award! And we hope that award comes in the form of a great career.

Reread this book. If you are reading this book before you start college, it should give you a jumpstart. Then read it again at the end of your first semester to jumpstart the second. Our advice will make even more sense then. The experience will be like taking your second trip to Paris—even better than the first.

GLOSSARY OF ACADEMIC TERMS

(Read the whole thing. You might learn something new.)

Academia or the academy. Sometimes the world of higher education is referred to as "the academy" or "academia." Example: *She worked in academia for decades before entering politics.*

Blue book. A small booklet of blank paper with a light-blue cover. These are sometimes used for writing the answers in essay-style exams. If the professor gives them out, it guarantees that the paper you use is clean and free from prior notes. If you are told to bring one for an exam, you buy it at your campus bookstore.

Catalog. A document colleges provide every year detailing majors, programs, course descriptions, academic rules, graduation requirements, and so forth that apply to the college as a whole.

College versus university. A college is a four-year, postsecondary school that offers courses that lead to a bachelor's degree. The students are called undergraduates. A university is a collection of schools or colleges, at least one of which offers graduate degrees such as a master's or doctorate.

Credit hours. The number of credits one earns by completing a course, usually measured in terms of "contact time" or hours in the classroom or lecture hall per week. Courses typically meet three hours a week and award three hours of credit. Labs tend to award one credit hour for three hours a week in the lab. It usually takes at least 120 credit hours for a bachelor's degree, including a minimum number of credits in your major.

Curriculum vitae (CV). This is a type of résumé usually used in the academic world. It tends to be longer than a standard résumé, listing publications, research interests, teaching experience, grants, awards, and anything relevant to academic accomplishments and skills.

Dean, provost, president. At a university, deans are in charge of schools, colleges, or special services such as dean of libraries or dean of students. The deans report to the provost who is in charge of the instructional and research missions of the university. The provost reports to the CEO, who is usually called the president.

Degrees. An associate's degree is granted at community colleges and takes a full-time student two years to complete. A bachelor's degree is an undergraduate degree granted by a college or university and takes a full-time student four years to complete. Graduate students pursue various degrees beyond a bachelor's degree at universities.

Department. Each subject area is organized in a department such as the English Department. You can usually major in any subject that has its own department.

Discussion sections. Some very large lecture courses meet at least once a week in smaller groups, usually led by a graduate student (called a teaching assistant or TA), for the purposes of discussing course topics or readings and to allow students the opportunity to ask questions.

Dissertation. The final project and paper produced as a requirement for a doctorate (PhD). It requires original research to be done as the basis for the written product.

Drop/add versus withdrawal. There is a short period at the beginning of each semester or quarter when students may drop a course, add a course, or both without any notation on the long-term record. After that period, if a student wants to drop a course, it is considered a "withdrawal" and is permanently recorded on the transcript, typically as a grade of "W" that does not get averaged into the grade point average, or GPA. Most colleges have a withdrawal deadline and rules about how many W grades you may receive.

Endowed chair. Some faculty members may have an additional title that reflects an honor and extra perks. For an endowed chair, a donor contributes a large sum of money that is invested by the university and the proceeds are used to support the research of senior-level professors.

Faculty. The academic staff (instructors and researchers) of the college or university.

Grade point average (GPA). The average of all grades for courses completed. (A=4, B=3, C=2, D=1, F=0.)

Graduate assistant (GA). A student who has already completed a bachelor's degree, is working on an advanced degree, and is employed as an assistant to faculty in teaching or research.

Grant. An award of money to support research by an individual faculty member or a group.

Hybrid course. A course that combines online and face-to-face instruction.

Incomplete. An incomplete, or "I," grade holds the place for a permanent grade until a student finishes a requirement such as the final exam or a paper. There is a deadline for completing requirements.

Learning management systems (LMS). These online software programs are supplied by colleges for tasks such as organizing course documents including the syllabus, recording grades, posting announcements, taking online assessments, and submitting assignments. The most common systems are Blackboard, Canvas, and Moodle. In online courses, the LMS is the place to find lectures and course discussion forums, too.

Mentor. An experienced and knowledgeable person who advises and models positive qualities for another person. If a student does a senior paper or works on research with a professor, the professor supports the growth and development of the student and would be considered a mentor.

Midterm exam. An exam that is important, but not the final exam. The term comes from the idea that it is an exam given midway through the course. But some courses give two or three "midterms."

Office hours. At most colleges, every instructor is required to hold office hours. These are stated times when students may stop by to talk to the instructor for any reason related to the class. You don't have to announce in advance that you are coming during these stated times.

Override. A permission for you to register for a course that is full or for which you need special permission (for instance, waiving prerequisites) in order to register. If a professor submits an override for you, the computer will allow you to complete the registration.

Peer-reviewed journal. A serial publication that contains articles written by experts in the field that are reviewed before publication by other experts to ensure correctness and substance of content, valid research methods, and original contributions to the field.

Plagiarism. The act of taking another person's work or words and passing it off as your own. It is fraudulent to do this.

Professional schools. Graduate schools that have programs to prepare students for a career in that profession at a level beyond a bachelor's degree. Examples include medical, dental, law, library, business, education, and more.

Reserve desk in a library. If your professor puts a book or other resource "on reserve" in the library, it means that it cannot be taken out of the building but may be used there for a limited time. You go to the Reserve Desk to check out the material. There is no guarantee that it will be available at the time you arrive as another person may be using it. Most libraries now have electronic reserves, but these sometimes still limit how many people can log on at once.

Rubric. A document that states what components should be included in your work and describes how levels of performance are scored. Not all assignments are accompanied by a rubric, but if it is, be sure to match your work to the requirements laid out in the rubric.

Sabbatical. Tenured college professors may be granted a paid sabbatical leave after about every seven years of regular employment. It means they are excused from their usual responsibilities, such as teaching and committee work, to pursue a project such as writing a book, doing research out in the field, or spending the year at another university doing research. It may be for a semester or two. The purpose is to allow the professor time to be creative and intellectually refreshed.

Semester versus quarter. Some colleges operate on a semester system that consists of two semesters per year of about fifteen weeks each. Others operate on a quarter system of three quarters per year about ten weeks each, plus an optional summer quarter. The more common system is semesters.

Seminar. A style of class in which assigned readings are discussed and debated. Various members of the class may take turns presenting material or leading the discussion. Class sizes tend to be small.

Syllabus. An academic document that lists course requirements and expectations for an individual course. See chapter 5 for more details.

Teaching assistant (TA). A graduate student who helps with a large lecture class or who staffs smaller break-out groups of the class or labs. The TA may be a grader for the class.

Tenure. Permanent appointment of a faculty member. Tenure usually is awarded at the time of promotion to the rank of associate professor. It means that the faculty member can only be terminated in extreme circumstances or for behaviors that are outlined in the policies of the college.

Terminal degree. A degree that is the highest one that can be earned in a field of study. It is most often a PhD, but could be a master's degree in a field that does not usually offer a doctorate such as a master of fine arts (MFA).

Transcript. The permanent record of your courses taken, grades, credits transferred from other colleges, and degrees earned. Keep an unofficial copy for your records when you graduate. For employment or grad school, you will need to have an official copy sent directly from the registrar of your college.

Undergraduate or undergrad. A student who has not yet attained a bachelor's degree.

REFERENCES

Atchley, Wayne, Gary Wingenbach, and Cindy Akers. "Comparison of Course Completion and Student Performance through Online and Traditional Courses." *International Review of Research in Open and Distance Learning* 14, no. 4 (October 2013): 104–16.

Carr, Nicholas. "How Smart-Phones Hijack Our Minds." *Wall Street Journal*, October 7–8, 2017, C1.

Clagett, Bob. "Bob Clagett on Taking a Gap Year." *College Admission*, March 20, 2013. http://collegeadmissionbook.com/blog/bob-clagett-taking-gap-year.

Kuznekoff, Jeffrey, Stevie Munz, and Scott Titsworth. "Mobile Phones in the Classroom: Examining the Effects of Texting, Twitter, and Message Content on Student Learning." *Communication Education* 64, no. 3 (2015): 344–65.

Lawson, Dakota, and Bruce Henderson. "The Cost of Texting in the Classroom." *College Teaching* 63 (2015): 119–24.

McConville, Mark. "How to Help a Teenager Be College-Ready." *New York Times*, July 26, 2018. https://www.nytimes.com/2018/07/26/well/how-to-help-a-teenager-be-college-ready.html.

Mueller, Pam, and Daniel Oppenheimer. "The Pen Is Mightier Than the Keyboard." *Psychological Science* 25, no. 6 (April 2014): 1159–68.

Nathan, Rebekah. *My Freshman Year: What a Professor Learned by Becoming a Student.* Ithaca, NY: Cornell University Press, 2005.

National Center for Education Statistics. "The Condition of Education." Updated May 2018. https://nces.ed.gov/programs/coe/indicator_ctr.asp.

Ophir, Eya, Clifford Nass, and Anthony Wagner. "Cognitive Control in Media Multitaskers." *Proceedings of the National Academy of Sciences* 106, no. 37 (September 15, 2009): 15583–87.

Sana, Faria, Tina Weston, and Nicholas Cepeda. "Laptop Multitasking Hinders Classroom Learning for Both Users and Nearby Peers." *Computers & Education* 62 (2013): 24–31.

van der Schuur, Winneke, Susanne Baumgartner, Sindy Sumter, and Patti Valkenburg. "The Consequences of Media Multitasking for Youth: A Review." *Computers in Human Behavior* 53 (December 2015): 63–70.